A Kingdom
Called Desire

A Kingdom Called Desire

CONFRONTED BY THE LOVE OF A RISEN KING

Rick McKinley

ZONDERVAN®

ZONDERVAN.com/
AUTHORTRACKER
follow your favorite authors

ZONDERVAN

A Kingdom Called Desire
Copyright © 2011 by Rick McKinley

This title is also available as a Zondervan ebook.
Visit www.zondervan.com/ebooks.

This title is also available in a Zondervan audio edition.
Visit www.zondervan.fm.

Requests for information should be addressed to:

Zondervan, *Grand Rapids, Michigan 49530*

Library of Congress Cataloging-in-Publication Data

McKinley, Rick
    A kingdom called desire: confronted by the love of a risen king / Rick McKinley.
       p. cm.
    Includes bibliographical references and index.
    ISBN 978-0-310-28543-4 (softcover)
    1. Spiritual life — Christianity. 2. Jesus Christ — Christianity. 3. Desire for God. I.
Title.
BV4511.M45 2011
  248.4 — dc22   2010049395

Published in association with Yates & Yates, www.yates2.com

Cover design: Aaron James, The Math Dept.
Interior design: Michelle Espinoza

Printed in the United States of America

11 12 13 14 15 16 17 18 19 /DCI/ 18 17 16 15 14 13 12 11 10 9 8 7 6 5 4 3 2 1

For my mom, Jacque,
You've always celebrated my desire for God

Contents

ONE

A Kingdom Called Desire

I have grown very tired of the question *how*. This question seems to permeate every inch of the world I live in. How-to books sell millions of copies every year promising that we can master a myriad of topics from weight loss to making it rich in the stock market. Every author gives us a different set of steps to take and makes promises to us that are never kept.

When we wake up feeling like crap again because we failed to climb the how-to ladder of success, in a matter of minutes we will see yet another commercial, infomercial, afternoon talk show, website, or news clip that points us in a new direction with another set of promises and steps to take to fix ourselves. The crazy part is we run to it like little kids running after the ice-cream truck in the heat of summer.

I am really tired of it, though. I am weary because the ice-cream truck never slows down for us, and after so many years I have begun to realize the truck didn't even have ice cream in it. It just played the carnival noises in the mega-phone and got us all excited, making us drop whatever it was we were doing and rush outside to catch our hopes and dreams, only to see the rear brake lights fading into the sunset. We just stood there with our handful of change and dissipating hope.

In many ways we have been robbed by the question of how. The question of how betrays us because it assumes the answers we long for are outside of us, held secretly by others, and only accessible for a small monthly fee. That's not true, though. There are no secret answers, only lived moments that create some type of personal knowledge.

That knowledge may have worked for one guy who lost weight and wrote a book. So we see that the guy who wrote a book on how to lose weight actually went from fat to thin — and he looks a lot happier and healthier — and we want that too, so we buy his book. I think I own all those books.

Those diet books contradict each other in many ways except one: they all tell you to eat less and exercise more. But most of us don't want to do that. Rather than doing the eat-less-move-more diet we hide behind an assumed ignorance. "I don't know how to lose weight." I don't have the answer. I need an expert to tell me how, and this skinny guy who used to be a fat guy has the answers I need.

We hide behind the question of how. *I've* hidden behind the question of how.

The betrayal isn't really in the question of how. The betrayal comes from a culture that has convinced us to look to someone else to find what we most deeply want. Some *thing* will make your life full or happy.

In one sense it's true: if you need to lose weight and you do, you will feel better; if you get out of debt, you will find freedom. I don't know how much the ShamWow will help your happiness, but after I watched the infomercial I really wanted it. A consumer

I am tired of the question *how*. I want to drill down deeper into my soul and ask a better question.

culture depends on us being paralyzed by the question of how in order for it to work. It creates a codependent relationship where we will endlessly clamor to the experts to tell us what we most deeply need. We must be honest, though. We are not much happier after years of seeking the experts' advice. In fact, most of us take our how-to books to Goodwill along with barely used exercise equipment we bought with great hopes that in just fifteen minutes a day our lives would be forever changed. Mine was called the Power Rider, and it made you go up and down like you were riding a bull or something, and I found riding it quite embarrassing, but not as embarrassing as when I think about how I bought it and just hung clothes on it for years until I threw it out.

So I am tired of the question *how*. I want to reclaim my freedom from having to ask it. I want to drill down deeper into my soul and the soul of our culture and ask a better question. The question may not have a simple answer or be able to be packaged and sold, but it may lead me to another question that takes me even farther into the deepest parts of me. Somewhere in there, somewhere in you, we may find a place where transformation resides and the person with whom it resides.

In his book *The Answer to How Is Yes*, Peter Block tackles this very issue and makes the observation that "good questions work on us, we don't work on them." He mentions that the right questions are about values, purpose, aesthetics, human connections, and deeper philosophical inquiry.[1]

Essentially he is saying the good questions are really about *desire*. What is it we most deeply want? Every advertisement taps into something deeper in you than your interest in the product. "If I had that I would enjoy my family more, I would embrace life with action, I would feel better about who I am, I wouldn't feel so ashamed, I would be a better dad, people would finally be impressed with me, I would feel like I made something of myself, my life would be easier, it would help me get out of my nowhere job . . ."

And the list goes on and on.

The list is endless because our desires run so deep and yet barely get touched by anyone other than advertisers seeking to get us to want what they are selling. So where does all of that desire go? I think it gets stuffed deep down inside us somewhere, because in a culture that has paralyzed us by convincing us we don't know how to do much in and of ourselves, desire scares us to death.

The good questions are really about *desire*. What is it we most deeply want?

---

1. Peter Block, *The Answer to How Is Yes* (San Francisco: Berrett-Koehler, 2003), 27, 39.

Why does desire scare us so much? Why is it that we go through the motions of living by trading our deepest desires for cheaper desires that we know are making promises to us they can't keep? Why do we run like kids after the ice-cream truck when we know it is empty or we'll never catch it? I wonder if we are afraid — afraid that when we touch that thing we desire, we won't know how to deal with it.

So let's say I think my desire is for my kids to be happy. I really want something more than that, but I am not sure what it is yet. So I settle for trying to make them happy. I wander around some dead ends for a while, buying them what they want and taking them where they want to go. But they still whine and complain. So then I listen to some expert who tells me that kids do better when they spend time with their parents. What they really need is time with me!

So I think about it awhile, then reset my schedule, making sure I'm home for family dinners and game night. I'm in the room with them, but it still feels as if something is missing. What is it? Is it me again? I am here, they are happy, but there is something more. Am I here emotionally and spiritually, or just physically? Are they content and do they have a deep sense of joy, or are they just happy because I bought them more stuff?

Then let's say I reflect some more and come to a place where I can actually name my deepest desire and embrace it: I love my kids! Nothing in the world can express the power of the love I feel for them. I feel that in me; I embrace it in me. Because of that love, I desire deep, personal, fatherly connection with my kids. Then something in me gets scared and is convinced I don't know *how* to make that deep connection happen. So I shun it or stuff it or avoid it, and — rather than creating my own story, together with my kids — in my fear of not knowing how, I simply rent another movie and try to enjoy someone else's story for the next ninety minutes or so with my kids.

Movies are fun, but they are not a substitute for making my own adventures with my kids. They are just a great way to hang out together on a Friday night. And this scenario repeats itself every day in every life. The question of how paralyzes me from just being fully present with my kids. In reality all I have to do is go do something, anything, pay attention, laugh, play, listen, make mistakes and memories, and feel that deep place fill with love.

So I am tired of asking how.

I am tired of cheap desires.

I am tired of avoiding the deeper desires.

One of the most damaging places for the question *how* is in our spiritual lives. The question itself has a place, but it should not be primary, and it should show up a ways down the road. The better questions, the ones that work on us and in us — those are the questions we need to deal with sooner.

In the West, Christians have leaned too heavily on the pragmatics of how. When we assume the answer we most deeply need is an answer outside of us that only an expert can give, we become a paralyzed people waiting to be told what to do next:

Go to church on Sunday? Check.

Belong to small group? Check.

Read Bible and pray daily? Check.

Wear appropriate Christian apparel, listen to Christian radio, home school, work in the soup kitchen, write letters to missionaries, take casserole to church potluck, drink fair-trade coffee, work to alleviate extreme poverty, eat vegetarian, recycle, sign human rights petition? Check, check, check, and check.

When we turn following Jesus into a product instead of a relationship, the only question we end up asking is, how do we do that? And we look for clues in what everyone else is doing and do that too. Pretty soon we are doing all sorts of things but we don't know why anymore.

When we turn following Jesus into a product instead of a relationship, the only question we end up asking is, how do we do that? And we look for clues in what everyone else is doing, and do that too.

I realize this is a tremendous oversimplification, but time and time again it comes back to haunt us. Truthfully a lot of the books we buy in regards to following Jesus are couched in this how-to language as well: Will someone out there tell me *how* to follow Jesus?

Jesus didn't spend a lot of time answering that question.

I find that to be really hopeful. When he did answer the how question, he did so in a way that was very personal to the one he was talking to. For example, a rich young ruler came and asked Jesus how to gain eternal life (Luke 18:18–27). Jesus told him to keep the commandments, to which the man basically replied, "Been there. Done that!" He had a checklist for salvation, licking his pencil as he marked off each step.

So Jesus masterfully tapped into the deeper question of desire in the rich young man's life. The question is: What are you really putting your security in? What do you really think is going to save you? For that rich young man, the answer was his own personal wealth and his ability to do the right things. That's where his security was. And when Jesus pointed out one area where the young man couldn't do the right thing, the man gave up.

In other places Jesus simply asked people, "What do you want?" or "Do you want to get well?" —questions that pushed right past the how-to questions and went directly to the issues most important to the person, the issues of desire.

"Do you really want to follow me or do you need your money to make you feel secure?"

"Do you want to be healed or do you need to be sick because you don't believe anyone will care about you if you are made well?"

The questions are deep, involved, not simple or reduced, and they cannot be packaged into a one-size-fits-all container. What do you desire most? Do you really want Jesus, or do you want beauty, a career, success, and happy relationships? Do you really want Jesus, or do you just want to fill in some boxes to prove that you are saved?

To the rich young ruler, Jesus said, primarily, "Come, follow me" (Luke 18:22). Get rid of the checklists. Stop thinking you can buy your way into heaven. Follow me. Quit asking *how* and starting asking *who*!

Sadly, I sometimes wonder if there is much of an audience for this type of spiritual undertaking today. We have traded in a great spiritual lifelong adventure with Jesus for religious chores that we can check off our list. The deeper questions that deal with the mystery of following Jesus— the parables that leave us puzzled, the art of *being* in Christ in a world of *doing* things for Christ, the dilemmas of pain and suffering—these questions get thrown out because we are too busy checking off our boxes, proving we are Christians. In throwing out the deeper questions we trade in the deeper desires for the cheaper ones.

Recently I have eliminated the question of how, especially in regard to following Jesus. I just quit asking that question. I am discovering and discarding my cheaper desires in order to pursue my deeper desires. I want a faith that isn't reduced, and I want to sit inside the questions Jesus and his kingdom cause me to ask and to sit inside the questions they are asking of me. I want to live into a new way

> **We have traded in a great spiritual lifelong adventure with Jesus for religious chores that we can check off our list.**

of being — because Jesus not only addresses our desires; he created them.

Transformation happens not through more how-to spirituality but by reclaiming our freedom so we can embrace the beauty and complexity of the kingdom of God. We have the freedom to realize we don't have to figure it all out or understand everything, but we can live in relationship with the living God through Christ.

Being who we were created to be in the midst of his kingdom and allowing Jesus to lead us to wherever he wants to take us ultimately will always make us come back to a place of desire, where our emotional life meets our faith and our reason in a beautiful way.

What I find in Jesus and his kingdom does not make me tired; instead he awakens me and invites me to learn to be and to become in ways unique to me. Jesus brings us freedom. We will know we are getting close to Jesus' kingdom when our deepest joy is confronted by our greatest fears. But if we press into those deeper questions, joys, and fears, they may open us up to the unlimited possibilities of living into the life of Jesus.

Some of our most difficult choices occur when we are unable or unwilling to admit that if the ice-cream truck is empty then we don't really know what we want. For me, realizing the truck will never stop at my house means I am left with some really big questions.

What if Jesus wants me to address a desire that is false? What if that false desire has become a safe place for me to live because I don't have to ask the deeper questions or examine the deeper places and desires within me? I can mask all of that by trying to figure out *how*—how to fix, how to change, how to understand, or how to master just about everything.

Instead Jesus asks me to embrace the life he has given me. He asks me to live that life out in the kingdom he has created. Tasks get turned into relationships and have-to's become want-to's, but all of it will remain at arm's length if I refuse to sit inside the question, what do I desire most? The question forces me to consider there is a distinct possibility that I don't desire God the most.

What do you want? What do you really want?

Isn't it weird that it's so hard to answer that question? Shouldn't we know the answer?

In Matthew 13, Jesus is teaching his followers about the kingdom. Halfway through the chapter we find one verse, one pregnant sentence that will ruin you if you really understand what he is talking about. It's the forty-fourth verse in the chapter, and it reads like this.

> "The kingdom of heaven is like treasure hidden in a field. When a man found it, he hid it again, and then in his joy went and sold all he had and bought that field."

Jesus places a picture of the kingdom before us—a picture of desire. In my most honest moment, this picture confronts my greatest fears with my greatest desires and opens up into a picture of his unlimited possibilities.

We see the kingdom tap into this person's deep desire: *A treasure hidden* . . .

We see the kingdom tap into perhaps his greatest fear: *Losing all he had* . . .

We see the kingdom confront that fear with something larger than all his fears.

We see his desire transformed before our eyes so that in his joy he goes and sells all he has to gain what he most deeply wants.

In a one-sentence parable I am invited to begin asking significant questions about my life, my heart, and my desire. Why don't I desire Jesus and the kingdom like that? What do I fear losing in order to buy this field? Why doesn't this scenario feel like joy to me?

But there hidden in my confusion over the parable is the story my heart is telling about what I desire.

I want security *now*, in this world. And my stuff, my things, my cash—they all give me a sense of security.

My heart isn't attracted to the kingdom like this man's was. What am I missing? What am I not seeing that he saw?

I really do put my trust in things I can touch and feel in the here and now. This invisible kingdom is hard for me to trust.

What happens if I sell everything I have to buy the treasure and it turns out to be disappointing?

What other thing in my life gives me this kind of joy?

What *would* I be willing to sell it all for?

The questions keep rising up from somewhere deep

within me, and I think Jesus wanted that to happen; in fact I believe he is behind the whole process. When I sit here in the midst of these questions—where my heart is confronted by Jesus' vision of the kingdom—something seismic takes place. I face up to the question Jesus is asking: What do you really want?

The kingdom does that to us. Jesus does that to us. Jesus wants us to sit with those questions, be driven to the Bible and to our knees with them.

What do you really desire? What do you really want? Take some time and think about that. Read that parable and chew on it awhile and jot down your own list of questions. What do I really want? Jesus is interested in your answer because Jesus is interested in becoming what you really want. "Sell everything you have. . . . Then come, follow me" (Luke 18:22).

Jesus answered that question for himself. He knows what he truly desires. In his joy he left all he had: the perfection of heaven, intimacy with the Father, the glory of glory. And he did it to buy a field that he purchased with his own blood, so he could have the treasure hidden within it.

You are the treasure in the field.

You are what he desires. Is he what you desire?

FORMATION QUESTIONS

1. Have you ever made a checklist of what makes you "Christian"? What is on that list?
2. In what ways has the question of how caused you to avoid what you really should be asking?
3. What are the top three cheaper desires that you find yourself wanting?
4. Read the parable of the hidden treasure again from Matthew 13:44. What do you think "selling everything you have" means for you?
5. What fear shows up inside of you when you think of losing that thing to gain the treasure?
6. Does it feel like joy to you to give it up to gain Jesus? If not, why do you think that is?

TWO

Love Moves Us from Duty to Desire

I remember sitting with my mentor in his office, which smelled of musty books, old and well read. For several years we met every Thursday at three o'clock. He was in his late sixties, a sage in my eyes. His eyebrows were thick and bushy, and when he talked about Jesus, his eyes would go big like he was seeing Jesus himself standing behind me. His prayers were never stale or pious or trite. When he prayed he was somewhere else, present to Jesus, his lover and Lord. I was happy just to breathe in the fumes of his passion for God.

At the time I was zealous and naïve, broken and frustrated. My questions often betrayed the depths of my spiritual ignorance. And my inner compass had moved from true north to due south. A spiritual journey that began with my heart responding to grace had quickly turned into a white-knuckle, willful attempt to pay Jesus back through a lifetime of duty.

I was failing at it. Three steps forward, two steps back, and after a few days I fell to a zero on a scale of one to ten. It might have been lust or greed or my temper going off. I am not sure which one it was that day, and it might have been all of the above.

It didn't take me long to veer off the path of responding to the grace given to me in Jesus and head down the path of works, striving to get God to like me by trying hard to obey him. The church had needs, the world had needs, there was a lot of sin and a lot that was broken, and I was happy to accept the job of making things — or people — right. And I was not overly religious in all of this, at least not outwardly.

But inwardly I was playing religious games as well as any Pharisee. In my mind, God had done his job, and now it was time to do mine. Without really knowing it or paying attention to it, I woke up most days hoping I could keep it together enough to get God to accept me.

My gospel was confused and I was either burning out or blowing up — and I'm not sure which it was, but I do know that it was subtle, not drastic. No grand tragedy, just a slow drift away from a relationship with Jesus driven by desire into a relationship based on duty. I ignored my heart and stuffed my desires.

So I sat with my mentor and bellowed on and on about this question and that question, all the time skirting around the central issue, which the wise man saw through quite easily.

Those large eyebrows squeezed together and his eyes

grew tight with concern. "Ohhhh, Rick," he said, with a deep sigh, looking away from me and staring out of his window, which looked out over the parking lot from his second-story office.

We sat for quite a while, and I started to squirm. You know that feeling deep in your stomach when you have been found out? That was the feeling. I had no idea what he was going to say next; I simply knew he was greatly concerned, not over an idea or a question I had asked, but for *me*.

He finally looked back at me, leaning forward with his huge eyes now in a squint, and as a grandfather would speak to a grandson, with a great and loving concern, he simply said: "God didn't call you to himself to use you, Rick. He called you to love you."

And then he leaned back in his chair. "God loves you, Rick."

I suppose I had heard that truth a few thousand times before, but this time I heard it. I really heard it.

Dutiful obedience done as a response to the love of God is a good work. Willful obedience done to gain God's approval and to earn his love is a religious work and is rooted in unbelief — and thus not a good work.

I had left that knowledge of God's love behind in my failed attempts to pay God back for my salvation. You can't earn grace, which is well defined as "God's love for us." Yet deep down I believed that because God had died for me on the cross, I needed to make myself approvable to him. Hence I was caught up in doing my duty.

Without knowing it, we often try to justify ourselves through our good works. Though many good works are a response to God's love, not all of them are. And some of them are done without a love for God at all. So simply doing good things is not a sign of spiritual security. A work is done for God only when it is done with the right motive, and many times our motives are decidedly mixed. Certainly when we do a good work to justify ourselves before God, it isn't a good work — it's heresy.

Dutiful obedience done as a response to the love of God is a good work. Willful obedience done to gain God's approval and to earn his love is a religious work and is rooted in unbelief — and thus not a good work.

I'm dumbfounded when I think how easy it was to become a person driven by religious work. Even when I began to wake up to my problem, I would often justify my religiosity. "God called me to help out here," I'd think. "He really needs me to get this mission going."

The old man's words pierced my self-importance, making me disoriented and uncomfortable. If his words were true, then all my work was fruitless. All my efforts to get Jesus to love me were of no use to him since he already loved me — and had even loved me when I sinned. If Jesus already loved me, I sensed, then my religious treadmill would lead to burnout, and I would become bitter with God and his people.

In fact I see a lot of people today who are bitter with

God, the church, or other believers. Most of those disillusioned people are living out the aftermath of not trusting Jesus and of trying to earn their salvation. When they couldn't save themselves, they blamed other people.

But if God called us to his love freely by grace and apart from works, then that love changes everything, because God called us to love us, not simply to use us.

I don't know that I fully understood it all that day. I'm pretty certain I didn't. God's love is one of those deep truths that takes a lifetime to apply. The beauty of God's love is so powerful and good that it continues to disorient us. It throws us off, then catches us as we are about to fall. God's love picks us up with all our broken pieces — our raw, sinful humanity — and begins to heal us with a gentleness, severe discipline, and kindness that keeps us clinging to Jesus, and not our own ability, as our only hope.

Duty can deceive us. Many things we do in the kingdom and for the King are motivated by duty. Somewhere inside of us we are captured by the reality that Jesus is Lord and we are not, and that moves us to serve, obey, and proclaim him. But the emotion fades, the vision falters, the desire dies out, and we begin to serve out of duty. Sometimes duty is all you have, because your desire gets twisted. Desire seems weak, so you fall back on duty. The season is dry, but you don't quit. You keep going, and much of this happens because you believe Jesus is worthy as your King. You serve him out of duty. Duty as a response to love is powerful. Duty as an attempt to earn God's love is destructive. Don't confuse the two. Duty that is a response to love is different than duty that is trying to get love to show up.

Duty might work for short periods, but it won't sustain you for the long haul. God called you to love you. Do you know what to do with that? Do you know how to respond to that? In the kingdom of God, people are growing comfortable and familiar with living into the love of God.

Duty as a response to love is powerful. Duty as an attempt to earn God's love is destructive. Don't confuse the two.

When the love of God seems like an idea instead of a reality, I find myself drifting into a duty mind-set. When I do this, I have a big problem, because I drift out of grace and away from the desire God placed in my heart. I end up feeling like following Jesus is a burden to carry, a goal to achieve, instead of a relationship to live in.

As a dad I do a lot of things for my kids simply because I am their dad. I go to work, I buy their clothes, I coach their games, I help with homework, I take them on vacation, I teach them things, and I discipline them when they disobey. All of those things sound like duties. But they are things I do because I am a dad. Before my children were born I was not a dad. Then I became a dad. I entered into a relationship with the four most amazing kids on the planet. I love them. I do what I do out of that relationship. It can look like duty but it's something much bigger than that. They made me a father, and I made them a son or a daughter. What I do for them is because of relationship, not duty.

Duty is dangerous. It looks good but it's deceptive. When duty runs out of steam, what will sustain you? But when your heart is growing in desire, then you will discover that God has an unlimited ability to fulfill your desire.

Love and duty are not competitors. In some ways they complement each other, but they are not equals either. Duty at its best is a response of love. When it becomes anything else you are at risk of perverting the entirety of your spiritual life. The Pharisees were dutiful, disciplined, and capable, but duty had taken an odd turn for them, and soon relationship with the lover of Israel was no longer part of their religious system, and their religious behaviors lost their spiritual meaning. The people Jesus frequently confronted were the most dutiful and religious people of his day. He confronted them with desire — the desire for a relationship with him.

The people Jesus frequently confronted were the most dutiful and religious people of his day. He confronted them with desire — the desire for a relationship with him.

I think of Nicodemus, a Pharisee and member of the Jewish ruling council who came to Jesus in the night so no one would see him (John 3). Despite his religiosity, Nicodemus became intrigued with Jesus. He was convinced God was with Jesus, and something inside Nicodemus desired God and wanted to understand God. But Jesus confused

Nicodemus with these words: "I tell you the truth, no one can see the kingdom of God unless he is born again" (3:3). "Born again" is a phrase that has become synonymous with crazy religious people, but it originated with Jesus speaking to a man who was already very religious. Jesus used the phrase to blow up Nicodemus's categories. Something only God could do would need to take place in Nicodemus's life: a new birth.

Nicodemus was wondering what God was up to — wondering what God required of him, why he would send someone like Jesus. Jesus announces to him that you cannot enter the kingdom of God unless you are reborn. And thus, duty-bound obedience hits its first roadblock. The question Nicodemus asks is: *How can I experience birth again? I am old. I have already been born.*

I assume Nicodemus had a duty problem like many of us do, because the question he wondered about was the same question our culture is fascinated with: How?

How can a man be born when he is old?

How can these things be?

I don't fault him of course. I would be asking the same things. Jesus blows up the categories of duty — categories that tend to work along the lines of . . .

How can I show you that I am a Christian? What do you want me to do?

How can I get into heaven?

How can I make sure you accept me?

How do I decide who's in and who's out?

When Jesus discards our duties as useless, then we are like people who've never been at sea who find themselves on the deck of a storm-tossed ship. We get seasick and stumble about at first, until we grow accustomed to the new way of being.

At first, like Nicodemus, we are confused, because Jesus is confronting duty with desire. He is scrambling the word *how* and turning it into *who*: How do I get into heaven? Answer: God so loved the world, he sent his Son.

In the kingdom of God we must be born of the Spirit, in the love of God, or we are not in the kingdom. God loves you, and doing your duty will never save you.

Back in my mentor's office I could feel the wheels of my duty-bound religion falling off. His gaze held God's love for me, and I sat there awkwardly, afraid to receive it. Standing face to face with my desire, I was confronted by my fear. Could I trust this love that was so excellent that nothing I could do for God would add anything to it? I wanted to believe the best news I'd ever heard, but I was afraid to trust. I was afraid to put the full weight of my heart on that reality. I don't know all the reasons why I was afraid, but I know I was.

My mentor sat in silence, waiting for my reply. In those quiet moments I began to realize what grace was: the love of God in the person of Jesus Christ. So powerful is love and grace that I could feel my heart attracted to the goodness and beauty of God. I was not trying to conjure up the emotions. My heart was apprehending the awesome reality of God at the core of his essence. God *is* love.

All I had tried to will myself to do was happening within me. I was not initiating; I was responding. The difference between the two is massive. I was not making this happen. God was alive, and in the perfection of his being and the power of his love, he was changing me.

I walked out of his office exposed. My head held my self-willed duty, and my heart held the love of God like a plastic cup trying to carry the sea.

Duty had been converted to desire by the Spirit of Jesus, who poured out his love into my heart through his spirit and the loving wisdom of a godly man. As I reflect back on that day I realize I still find it easier sometimes to believe God called me to use me rather than to love me. It's safer, it's quantifiable, it's something I can control, but I know when I go there that I am moving away from Jesus and the kingdom, and the love of God pulls me back.

Duty without love turns us into workers without relationship. Instead of seeing ourselves as beloved sons and daughters of a heavenly Father who adores us, we become servants of a harsh and distant King.

We all have the propensity to try to be God or play God. I even try to play God in my relationship with God! But I am just a sinful object of holy love. I am not even able to initiate a response to Jesus without the assistance of his Spirit.

So Jesus is effecting a deep change inside of me. Desire

for Jesus is defining me. When he manages to display his kingdom through me, that is nothing more than an overflow of his love, which I have cultivated in authentic desire. The kingdom of God is displayed not simply in the good works of God's people, but in love personally owned in the heart of his children and overflowing into the world for his glory.

Duty without love turns us into workers without relationship. Instead of seeing ourselves as beloved sons and daughters of a heavenly Father who adores us, we become servants of a harsh and distant King. We toil away down in the servants' quarters, but we never come up to the party with the fattened calf and the flowing wine.

Jesus called you to love you, not to use you. He wants you to desire *him*, not the duties you can do for him. He wants you upstairs at the banquet, feasting on his love.

FORMATION QUESTIONS

1. Is it easier for you to be wanted or needed? Why?
2. What role does duty play in your relationship to Jesus?
3. Name some ways that you try to pay God back for saving you.
4. How does it feel knowing God called you to love you, not to use you?
5. In what ways is love more powerful than duty in your relationship with Jesus?
6. What are some things in your faith that would change if you were driven by God's love for you rather than by duty?

THREE

The Problem with Desire

One of the first lessons I learned at church was not to be honest. Of course I did not learn that lesson from the man behind the pulpit, nor did I find that lesson in the Bible. Instead, like most important lessons, this one came through experience.

A couple of weeks after I started following Christ, I realized two things in my previous life were going to have to go: getting drunk and having sex. At the time, heaven sounded like payday, so I figured my reward for my newfound sobriety and celibacy would be getting back everything I'd had to give up. So in my exuberant ignorance, I asked the college pastor if heaven was like the greatest party ever, with all the drinking and sex you could imagine.

My frame of reference was clearly rooted in my understanding of pleasure and rewards and the hopes and dreams of an eighteen-year-old boy-man. The only experience of ecstasy I had ever had that resembled anything of the ecstasy waiting for me in heaven was getting drunk and having sex.

I honestly think that is how most eighteen-year-old boys think, raised in the church or not. But the college pastor looked at me in horror, as if I had trampled on something sacred and defiled something holy. He was right to think that. Drunken orgies in heaven would be unholy and quite defiling of something sacred. Yet the desire I had for an eternity of ecstasy was in fact legitimate. I had experienced ecstasy as momentary (and painful the next morning), but I longed for something better, something lasting and life-giving.

In my exuberant ignorance, I asked the college pastor if heaven was like the greatest party ever, with all the drinking and sex you could imagine.

Through that experience I learned that honest questions developed from limited life experience were frowned upon, at best, and better left unspoken. An honest question — horrific as it was to my holy friend's ears, though spoken in innocence — created a reaction that made me feel like a stupid person asking a stupid question. So I quit asking questions. I muted my rage, repressed my desire, and learned: don't be honest here.

I later found out that there were several men in that church that I respected and had been taught by who had been living out the dreams of my eighteen-year-old passions — only not with their wives. In fact they hid behind a string of lies. But, given the first rule of religious living that I'm quite sure they learned as young children growing up in church — which is *don't be honest* — they just waited for everything to implode so they could crawl away from their respective disasters in shame. Yet I know something they now know and most people never get a chance to know: we never find freedom until we are ready to be honest.

Honesty is the place where freedom begins, when we are done pretending to be something we are not. God loves honesty.

Eighteen-year-old boy-men *should* be able to equate heaven with a fifty-keg party and dancing naked women who want nothing more than to sleep with them over and over until the sun rises on their fatigued bodies and there are no STDs and no hangovers.

What if an older man would listen and affirm the desire underneath the desire? Then he could point this young rutting bull in the direction of marriage and fidelity and getting a job, so he can make love to a woman who will make him feel like heaven is real and the love of God is tangible. Then these two can lie naked and unashamed on their wedding night and feel the blessing of God over their marriage bed. They can keep practicing for years to come and realize sex can get better even when bodies start to look older and gravity rears its head. And no matter how great sex is, the older man must point out, this young rutting bull will still desire something deeper than sex with this woman he holds. He will long for an even deeper intimacy, which is a longing for God. And that is a longing for heaven, which is not a fifty-keg party with naked women but the most intimate, loving experience any of us will ever have. The only thing close to it is the love between a man and a woman in marriage. What the young man really desires is for God to put the world right and to make him new again.

And so you see, underneath that horrifying but honest question was a real desire that shouldn't have been stuffed but redirected — a desire from the heart that needed to be pointed toward God and coached along the way.

As shocking as honesty can be, underneath it is something redeemable. Honesty creates a context for freedom and defeats shame. Honesty removes us from isolation and reminds us that we are human. The struggles of that young man, honestly spoken, should help that older man keep his own pants on and get to work at loving his own wife.

Being honest about desire is important, because our longings for God typically go unmet. Our desires show up like a shoot coming out of the ground, and that's what we see and pay attention to: the desires we can name, feel, or want — like the desire to have sex, to look good, or to be successful. But beneath the surface — at the roots, where the heart is searching for the thing to attach our affections to — that is where a desire for God lies.

When we are not honest about the lesser desires, the weedy stalks and stems kind, the desires for fame and fortune and beauty, then we never get to the roots of our desire.

At our core we desire something larger, deeper, more significant, transformational, intimate, and unconditionally loving. A deeper essence to life, a stronger flavor to existence, a lasting touch that opens up into embrace. Those are the desires that God is deeply interested in us being honest about, because those are desires for God.

When we are not honest about the lesser desires, the weedy stalks and stems kind, the desires for fame and fortune and beauty, then we never get to the roots of our desire. Beneath the surface and past the behaviors, into the heart.

So, what do you want? What do you really, really want? Look at the people and things that you give yourself to, the sins you keep coming back to. What do they tell you about your desires? What about your passions, the life-giving moments that you share or participate in: What do they tell you about what you want? Are they attached to sin or are they good and very good? They both tell us the story of our hearts.

So, what do you want?

Just asking the question can make us stumble. What if I face that desire and I realize that what I desire I can't have? Or realize that I don't desire what I do have? What if I desire freedom and I am a stay-at-home mom with three kids under the age of five? What if I desire passionate sex and I am married to that stay-at-home mom with three kids under five and she is tired? What if I want my daughter not to have cancer? What if I want to be married and I don't think anyone will ever be interested in me? What if I don't desire God? What if I desire freedom from God?

What if . . .

The questions keep rolling because fear lurks behind the veil of our hearts and honesty pulls back the veil revealing our desires. Do we dare to be honest with God about our deepest desires?

Some desires, on the other hand, are immediately freeing. I desire Jesus, I desire to be creative, I desire to love another, I desire to do justice and love mercy, I desire to serve ...

Desire is never neutral, but it's often stunted by the fear of being honest. But you must be honest. Don't worry how it sounds. Be honest — desire demands it.

Honest desires are windows into your soul, and however ugly they are to think about and even more horrific to speak aloud, they have underneath them an ultimate desire God can redeem.

I hope you will realize that those honest desires are windows into your soul, and however ugly they are to think about and even more horrific to speak aloud, they have underneath them an ultimate desire God can redeem.

The desires may be buried and the desires may be sinful, but until we are honest about them, we will never find the freedom that Christ invites us to in the kingdom. So keep digging. God has created you with an ultimate longing for him, and underneath the ugly things you do to fulfill that longing with substitutes, there is a real desire for God or there isn't, but you will never be satisfied until you find out. I think there are a lot of miserable people acting religious who don't want anything to do with God. It would be good to admit that if that's you. You are not helping anyone by living out of a fractured faith.

Be honest and let the chips fall where they may. We were not given life to waste it trying to be nice and good; we were given life to live passionately for Jesus and his kingdom. You have to refuse to let your life be reduced to the opinions of the critics, bystanders, and paparazzi of Christian living. Let us be a people who are willing to be honest for the sake of our souls and our children. They need to see authentic faith.

Life in the kingdom is defined in part as an honest life. Otherwise living in the kingdom is reduced to people who have received forgiveness and now are trying to pay God back by trying to be good people. This is unsustainable and passionless, and it's heresy. We can't fake this radical life of following Jesus; it must flow from a place of honesty.

In truth, we are afraid to face the reality that in the depths of our desires we don't desire Jesus and his kingdom. So we ignore those places only to realize we are once again in a pattern of trying hard and failing, without hope that we will be able to change our course.

It is good that we keep failing.

I think Jesus ensures that we keep failing. Because if we could mask the deeper places in our soul where desire is formed and given voice, then we would be at risk of missing everything Jesus is and desires to carry us into.

I think Jesus wants us to sit in the deeper places of our soul for a while. He invites us to look at our desires — those real desires that represent in some way where the affections of our hearts lie. So why do we keep avoiding being honest about them?

I think we don't want to be found out. We want to appear as though our faith is working, and we resist the honest examination of our hearts because of what we might find there. The psalmist prayed a bold prayer asking God to search him and know him and find out what is going on in the deep places of his heart (Psalm 139:23). Are we willing to pray that prayer?

Dishonesty is not simply about hiding sinful deeds or beliefs or doubts from others who we fear will judge us or reject us. Those are powerful fears, but ultimately they are only the smaller fears inside a much bigger fear, which is fear that *God* would find us out. We deceive ourselves into believing that we can hide these off-putting desires from God — which we can't — but as long as we don't admit to them and keep swinging hard for our faith, we think that even God will not notice.

At the intersection of honesty and desire we begin to realize that desire is ultimately a quest for life. Desire can manifest itself in a number of ways, good or bad, but the end game is the same: we are longing and looking, seeking and striving for life. We want more.

Here our quest becomes problematic, because our desires lead us to the discovery that the very thing we long for, we do not possess in the ultimate sense. Life at the fullest and most secure place is just outside our grasp.

Life leaks out of us. We age, we fail, we get sick, we lose loved ones—all of which point us to the fact that the life we desire is impossible to secure. Our hearts want love, intimacy, comfort, security, power, control—all of which express themselves relationally—but those affections, if not captured by God, will latch themselves onto idols.

Because we are essentially relational, we most deeply desire a community of love where we are accepted and known and loved no matter what. But our desire for deepest intimacy is inevitably spoiled, because our relationships will not always meet our expectations, and therefore our desires will go unmet.

Yet it is possible to mask this core disappointment. In the Western world, especially, we tend to reduce our desire to something simple, like financial security or having a career that fulfills us. If we can reduce our desires, then for the most part we are satisfied.

Spiritual desire can likewise be reduced. The tendency to believe Jesus' job is to meet all of our material needs but not capture our heart distorts our view of desire and God. If our faith in God is dependent upon living at a certain financial level in order for us to believe God is good, we are chasing a false gospel. We need a deeper spirituality and therefore a deeper desire. Any answer to our spiritual hunger that requires us to live in an affluent country for our faith to be real will not suffice.

Paying attention to our hearts brings us face-to-face with a hunger and thirst for life.

So when we face what we really want and we take the risk to be honest with ourselves, others, and God about those desires, we need to dig a bit deeper past the fray of *things* and *stuff* in order to get to the heart's desire. We don't simply want a better job; we want security and fulfillment and meaning. We don't just want better sex; we want passion and ecstasy; we want to be desired and to desire. We don't just want to be married; we want to love and be loved — united in a bond of intimacy and faithfulness. We don't just want the smaller desires; we want *life*.

Paying attention to our hearts bring us face-to-face with a hunger and thirst for life. And right here we may become the most afraid, because honesty that is willing to admit what we truly desire must also admit life is not completely ours to possess. In fact, life is quite limited.

All around us life is dying; therefore, life is insufficient. It thrives and blooms from generation to generation, and yet it is simultaneously like a vapor and a breath, a grass that is here one day and withers away the next.

We want more. We want life that is more than this, that won't fade, that can endure and will ultimately satisfy in perfect love and goodness. But that life is nowhere to be found within us or in this world.

So we seek it out from outside of ourselves. But soon the things and relationships quickly show their true colors, and we recognize there is still more that our hearts long for. We're never satisfied. How can that be? How can you have it all and still want more? The house, the car, the kids, the spouse, the friends, even faith, and the heart desires *more*? Could it be that the heart was made to be satisfied by that which only Jesus possesses? Life that isn't just in him, but *is* him.

If this wasn't true then you would never see the successful CEO or pastor who risks everything and loses their family and career, exchanging it for a sordid affair. He wanted more. Or the famous musician who had wealth and fame who dies after overdosing. What were they still looking for? We all want more.

> **We're never satisfied. How can you have it all and still want more? The house, the car, the kids, the spouse, the friends, even faith, and the heart desires *more*? Could it be that the heart was made to be satisfied by that which only Jesus possesses?**

Some may argue that this is not true. In fact, many people feel pretty sure they are just a few more items away from having everything they want, and their hope is banking on that last missing piece. Once it is put into place, they believe, life will be all they most deeply desire. Think Commodity God here. These folks banking on the missing pieces tend to see God as a resource who will broker their cheap desires. When he does, he is good. If he doesn't, he is bad.

God is the key resource to getting that last piece in place. That man, these kids, that cure, the next promotion, getting my wife to be who I want her to be — you may think you are just a few steps away from it all coming together.

But here is what I would tell you: *you are not being honest*. All of the material wells eventually run dry. The lesser things you desire may not be bad. In fact, most of those desires are very good, but they are also insufficient. Right here with your very good desire you are at the greatest risk. When that good desire becomes to you the key that will open the fountain of life, then it is replacing what your heart was made for with something only earth contains. In the place of your longing for life beyond this world, you have created an idol made up of the stuff of earth. And that's being dishonest to yourself at the very core of your being.

To face this takes a great amount of courage, pushing through the very tangible but insufficient things to face a desire that you can't capture by yourself or for yourself. To admit that you can't do anything to justify your life.

But this is also the place of salvation. Only God can give you the life that you were made for. Only Jesus can justify your life. The one who existed outside of this world, but entered into this world, the one who created life, but gave up his life, is the one who justifies your life with his blood shed on the cross. Jesus gives us his life by his spirit.

When you realize that the life you long for needs to come from Jesus and not this world, then you are free to treat people differently. You begin to allow your loved ones to be who they are without expecting them to meet your heart's desire for life in its fullest form. As you embrace them as they are, you learn not to place them in a position where they will always disappoint you. You enjoy their presence and what they offer without demanding more or asking them to be something they can never be.

But what about this desire and longing for life? Being honest allows you to hear Jesus' teaching with new ears, to see his life through new eyes. Being honest allows you to admit with open hands that you need what you don't possess and you were made to long for something that earth does not contain.

If this is true, life then must be redefined and ultimately revealed. If earth cannot contain life, then something outside of this world must have it, and someone must show it to us. Once we find that we can't satisfy our own desires, then we discover to our dismay that we are very weak and quite dependent. We need God to reveal life and give us life, because ours is failing, but our hearts won't accept less than the life we know we were created for. Those whom God has made for himself simply will never be satisfied with the dying life that we have at our own disposal. Our hearts, open and honest, long for something more.

FORMATION QUESTIONS

1. If you were to be honest about your faith right now, what would you say?
2. Can you describe a time that reinforced for you the "rule of religious living" that you shouldn't be honest?
3. What fears do you have about being honest about your life with another person?
4. What fears do you have about being honest about your life with Jesus?
5. What would freedom look like for you if you could be honest?

FOUR

Life and Death

An intimate hush weighs heavy in the air at every funeral I have ever been to. All of those who are sitting in the audience feel it. The photos of the person who is no longer with us scroll across the screens at the front of the room. Music plays quietly and tears flow freely as the hugs are held out to comfort us. Because the one we loved has gone before us, we know that we are not exempt from our own day. We all sit together bearing the wound of our mortal humanity represented in the person we loved and are saying good-bye to. Death. What I desire in those moments is that death would not exist.

Although we may long to tap into the deeper places within us, obstacles act as roadblocks to our interior lives. One of those obstacles is death.

Almost everything we do is an attempt to ensure that life continues. Avoiding death may not be at the forefront of our thinking, but in the end that is why we do much of what we do. We don't want to simply exist; we want to thrive.

And death is standing there threatening all that we are and hope for, because like a terrorist it destroys the very thing we have been trying to maintain: life.

Still, something within me needs to face death, even though I find the whole idea of death so toxic I want to pretend it's not there. But we desperately need to get in touch with its reality and presence.

We live in a culture that makes it easy to avoid our approaching appointment with death. We can manipulate our appearance so we don't look like we are aging. Inject some Botox, get some hair plugs, airbrush some pictures. Why would we do all that? Sure, we want to look good. But I think something else is going on. We don't want to admit that our aging bodies are proof that death is approaching. Sometimes death comes tragically and unannounced, but most of the time we walk step-by-step toward it.

The four Gospels are honest about death. The focal point of all four is the death of Jesus. There is no avoiding the subject when you read through Matthew, Mark, Luke, and John. Jesus talked about his own death and recognized that death is a great enemy that we have no power to fight on our own.

Jesus invites us to take death head-on and face its reality in order that we might know how deeply we desire life. But we instinctively want to avoid death, and when we do face its raw reality we find ourselves asking uncomfortable questions about God and his world, like: Why do I have to suffer and die? Why is there so much pain in the world? Why do the innocent suffer while the wicked prosper?

As I turn to face death's reality, which is here all around me, I have to face the fact that I don't like the story God wrote. It requires too much of me. It doesn't satisfy me quickly enough, and the brutal honesty isn't all that helpful either. For

Jesus invites us to take death head-on and face its reality in order that we might know how deeply we desire life.

the life of me I can't figure out why we all have to die. I get it, we sinned. That's awful, and we deserve it.

But it is maddening to face suffering and death. Death lurks like a dragon at the bottom of a chasm that you can never cross. Time stands behind you with a prod pushing you year by year, day by day, minute by minute, breath by breath closer to the edge of the uncrossable canyon. When you finally have no more ground, you fall off and get devoured. Death, like a dragon flaunting his victory, stands in the midst of carcasses swallowed and bones spat out.

I used to like the story. I was younger; life was tamable. I loved the glory of Jesus Christ, the power of the cross. I followed boldly. I still love it, but it is different now; the uncrossable canyon is in sight, changing how I understand living. The longer I followed Jesus, the more I wondered where he was taking me. And then I became aware that he was not simply showing me how to live but also how to die.

I didn't like that. I don't like that. So something clicks

inside of me and I question if I can trust him. Can you trust Jesus if he leads you where you don't want to go?

I start to talk to him less and question his direction more. The paths we keep going down — more often than not — I wouldn't describe as fun. These paths change me, but often through pain. Jesus just doesn't stop messing with the deepest places within me, the places I think I've buried or forgotten.

These paths lead me to the uncrossable canyon. In a small clearing, I notice it: this huge canyon ahead of me with Jesus on the other side. I look down and see the dragon, with its flaming mouth gaping wide and bones of previous travelers strewn about. The creature is Death. The path ends here. No bridge to cross. No way out.

But Jesus is across the way, beckoning me to trust him. He will raise me up after I die.

This is ridiculous, I think to myself. *What kind of spiritual journey is this? I don't like this story. I don't want anyone to hurt, suffer, or die. But I can't fix the story. We all die. I can't save myself or anyone else.*

I stand staring at the creature, but it's not my time to die. I stare across at Jesus and he stares back at me. It is as if he is saying death is not optional. He can sense my protest within my stare. This is where the story leads.

I don't have to die physically. Yet. But I do have to die, to self. I do have to die by faith before I ever face my own death.

I thought this was the author of life.

I resist. I turn and begin to cut my own path along the edge of the canyon hoping for another path, a way around or across. The creature is always present but not presently interested, and Jesus is standing firmly where he was — fading in the distance, quiet, not chasing or calling, just simply letting me go.

There has to be a better story. A different path. Through thickets and brush I trample on, never finding another path, never finding another bridge. I have to fix this, but I can't fix it. I am screwed.

I wanted to cling to one part of the gospel: his death for me. I don't want to grapple with the implications of *my* death in him.

Hope withers because the one who is my only hope in death is the one I just walked away from. This place is barren of hope. So I give up and head back to the path where I departed from Jesus. Instead of plunging into death by faith I turn back and try to return to days gone by. I invest myself as I did in the early days of simple grace, the zealous passion for evangelism, the righteous quest to reform church in a more meaningful and missional way. But nothing works.

It doesn't work because Jesus is not here; I walked away from him. I walked into some religious-looking activities, but I still walked away — not wanting to face the challenging place he took me to. Not wanting to face death.

I wanted to cling to one part of the gospel: his death for me. I don't want to grapple with the implications of *my* death in him. I don't want to have to wrestle with my doubts about my own resurrection. I just want him to forgive me, help me, give me heaven on earth. Keep my family safe and healthy, happy and secure. And bless my work for him. I want life without death.

But Jesus gives life *through* death.

Jesus isn't disinterested in our family's health, in taking care of us, or in blessing our work; he is simply not satisfied with those things in the same way we are. He isn't interested in a life without death-conquering power or grave-defeating courage and hope.

So I return to the place where I had been led, the place where Death lurks. The same dragon is waiting to devour me when I am forced into the uncrossable canyon. The same invitation is on the table: "Take up your cross and follow me. I am the resurrection and the life."

Some people have no problem with this juncture. Apparently my inner life is more messed up than theirs, because I don't like this story. I don't know why he who writes with sovereign pen has allowed this part of the play to invade our lives like this. I want something easier, simpler, cheaper, and more accessible.

I think of the sweet innocence of my daughter's trust. I wonder if this is true for her. Will she peacefully one day, with childlike faith, slip off the cliff through death into the arms of Jesus? Will she be full of fear? Will I be there to hold her, or will I have gone on before her?

Now I wonder if I am tackling a subject too big for me. I am no C. S. Lewis or N. T. Wright. I don't have the patience to wordsmith this to death. I am just a pastor, who is not much of a follower of Jesus and who doesn't want to move forward. I want time to stop. I don't want my kids to grow any older; I don't want my wife and me to get older. I am not ready for this. I hate this story. I don't have the faith to move through it. I can't stop it. I can't stop it. I can't . . .

I am not really living the brief life I have been given.

I don't think many of us are.

Or maybe that's not fair. Who am I to say that?

I just know I miss a lot.

Making peace with God — Jesus did that for us by his grace, through death. It's a death I deserved. I still deserve it, but in grace he has given me new life. New life, encased in a dying body.

Until the body dies, the new life cannot rise.

This is true both physically and spiritually.

Fairness assumes that God owes us something. I don't think that's true. I think we owe everything to God, and he owes us nothing.

I have made an idol out of this life. I like it better than what is to come. (Then again, maybe that's not true; there is a ton I hate about it.) But love — love that I have for my wife, my kids, this powerful love: it moves me to feel something so deep I can't explain it. When death shows up, the object of love disappears. Love equals pain. Why love when they only disappear?

I can't stop them from going. I can't stop my own death. I can't make this life better. God is there; of course he is there. I am not certain what he thinks of all my protest. It is not simply the unfairness of it. I don't think fairness is the issue. Fairness assumes that God owes us something. I don't think that's true. I think we owe everything to God, and he owes us nothing. That's what makes the incarnation, atonement, and resurrection so miraculous.

I am protesting two things right now. I protest that I am not in control of the story, and I protest the challenge that lack of control brings to my faith.

Hope, then, is something of a by-product of faith. It shows up unannounced. You can't conjure it up or produce it. Hope is the beautiful cousin that shows up at the party and makes the whole place shine. You didn't think she was coming, but she showed up with Belief. Since Belief came, Hope came. And Hope is beautiful.

That is the emotion of hope.

But there is a place to focus our hope. We can point it toward someone and set our gaze there. When we focus our hope in God, he has everything to fulfill what our hearts deeply want.

I am too easily satisfied. I will take a cheap hope any day. Advertisers love me because I laugh at their stupid commercials, but I buy their trinkets. Some of them are larger than life: cars, houses, electronics. They bring me hope. A new album, the perfect book, a great cup of coffee. Apparently I don't need much. Just a bit of icing on the cake of life, which is already pretty good.

I don't dare to imagine children dying because they don't have clean water or people suffering under the hand of a brutal tyrant committing genocide. That pretty much screws up the whole thing for me.

I am sure people who suffer must like resurrection more. That friggin' dragon has them by the neck most of the time.

But that doesn't answer anything for me. The plight of humanity doesn't make death easier; it makes it more complicated.

I hate the story.

Perhaps that's too strong. I like the good bits and hate the bad ones. I find the reality of love the most powerful and amazing thing. Love is dangerous, and at times I am afraid to touch it lest I be consumed. I can't get over the intimate relationships of family, friends, and neighbors. Relationships define us and confront us. They have power to them. It's not always a good power; at times it's a damaging power, but a power nonetheless. The power of love is as dangerous as the power of death.

So I can't say I hate the story completely. But I find it impossible to believe death is part of it. Of all the possible worlds that could have been created, the infinite wisdom of God created this one with the possibility of horrific problems. My hope in God is shaken, but I still believe he is in control. I believe he created this world, and it brings him great glory and is for our joy, but I just can't figure out how that works right now.

Facing the obstacles that keep us from fulfilling our desires can threaten and unnerve us, but don't be afraid of facing them. In these questions we begin to see what really is going on in our hearts and our faith, and there God can meet us in honesty. And that is a great way to meet with God. No more pretense or pretending, just our hearts bare before him as they always are, and God revealing himself to us in profound ways.

I hate the story in the same way because I can't see the whole picture right now, so it doesn't make sense to me. I am simply a character in the play arguing with the author that he shouldn't kill my character off because I have a lot to offer yet. I am not so much

What do I fear, and why does that fear keep me from the depths of what I most deeply want?

interested in the way the whole story weaves together into a glorious redemption; I am just trying to protect my bit. I am more like a talent agent threatening to sue the writer for not giving me enough lines. But the author of this story is writing something beautiful, and one day I will stand in awe as the credits roll and I see what it all means.

When I can let him write the story, the first thing I find is that it really is not about me being honest with God. He knows what is going on in my heart much better than I do. This is about me getting honest with me.

What do I fear, and why does that fear keep me from the depths of what I most deeply want?

Heavy question, but it's the right question. This is not about avoiding the question of death, but about facing it head-on and trusting the gospel to pull me through not only the question but death itself.

Hating the story because death is a part of it shows me something really important. Deep down I protest the reality of death because I know it doesn't belong. It was not meant to be. And I don't simply know this because the Bible told me; I know this implicitly, instinctively.

Death does not belong here.

Just because I don't like it, or don't understand why God allowed death to reign in this world, doesn't mean I shouldn't ask the hard questions of my own heart, faith, and God. In turning to face my desire, I begin to learn that the Spirit of God does some of his most deeply transforming work in the midst of the questions we have been too afraid to ask.

I don't like death, because I love life. And what I love most about life is the presence of love. Death is the obstacle to life and love, and I can't seem to find this lasting love here on earth. C. S. Lewis said it best in *Mere Christianity*: "If I find in myself a desire which no experience in this world can satisfy, the most probable explanation is that I was made for another world."[2] So then I find in this fear of death the evidence of God. In protesting death I realize that I was made for another world, because I long for life beyond what this world can contain.

I long for a place where death does not exist, because I am longing for life. The very thing that causes me to shrink back from life is the possibility that I may lose it. Yet, in protecting life, I squelch it of the most powerful evidence that it exists: the ability to desire love — to love another, to be loved, and to experience the untamed and shameless state of love I was originally created for.

Death stands mockingly over that, and I am at a crossroads.

I can face death's reality and live unbridled into life, passionately loving people from the depths of who I am while I know full well that death will come and rob them from me and me from them, rearing its ugly head in the midst of our relationship. Or I can retreat. I can stuff the desire for life. I can cling and protect and live life with a half-hearted limp. And this, I think, is right where God wants to meet us, at the border edge of the kingdom of heaven.

Don't fear this obstacle of death in the face of your desire. Instead turn to it, wrestle it down, ask the hard questions, and wait on the King. It would be a shame if we missed God's deepest transforming work because we

2. C. S. Lewis, *Mere Christianity* (New York: Macmillan, 1960), 120.

assumed we were not supposed to talk about the deepest and most important parts of our hearts.

The one who stands across the canyon, seen through the smoky haze from the breath of that creature Death, has promised that before I fall into the creature's claws I will be rescued by the nail-pierced arms of death's conquering love. For this beast limps about trying to have his way over our hearts and minds, but he has been defeated by the man on the other side.

FORMATION QUESTIONS

1. In what ways does our culture try to hide the reality of death?
2. In what ways do you avoid accepting the reality of death?
3. What are some of the cheaper desires that people chase after to help them avoid thinking about death?
4. The author talked about not liking the fact that in God's story we all have to face our death. Do you resonate with that?
5. How does facing death openly help you to tap into your deeper desires?
6. Does Jesus' victory over death give you hope? Why or why not?

FIVE

The King of Life

Listen . . . Listen to life.

Life pulsates around us. The chirping of birds out my window, the warmth of sunlight finally breaking through winter's grey blanket, the cars that speed up the hill, the chaotic noise of advertisers, the rush of shoppers at the mall, and workers on the freeway driving in and out of the city. Life is crashing, whispering, pulsing beneath our skin, but too often it goes unnoticed. It becomes white noise in the back of our head like the fan that runs all night while you sleep.

Jesus made it a priority to call us to attentive living, not simply allowing this miracle of life to go by unnoticed. The polarizing realities of death and life are central to our existence and our salvation. Each night we lie down to sleep and each morning we rise again. This daily pattern that repeats itself in nature's seasons and our normal workday points to the ultimate reality of death and life. To ignore either of them is to miss the miracle that Jesus pronounced over both death and life. Conquering the first and giving us the second.

In the middle of the brutal reality of death, Jesus never stopped calling people to life. Centering his attention on life, he continually pushes past the smaller and cheaper things we tend to live for and goes right to the core issue, which is life itself.

Death and life show up repeatedly in the Gospels. Jesus is always contrasting them in paradoxical fashion. If you want to save your life, then give it up. If you cling to life, you lose it (see Matthew 16:25).

The core necessity of kingdom living is to possess, desire, and be empowered by a different life from our own. Jesus is never interested in restructuring the life you currently have. That can happen through any self-help program, and by the looks of the best-seller list, people seem to be devouring the advice.

Jesus is never interested in restructuring the life you currently have. That can happen through any self-help program.

The problem seems to be that we are not quite ready to give up the life we currently have. We cling to it and hope to improve it. For many people, following Jesus into his kingdom is simply putting a polish on a broken spirituality. Instead of simply sitting by and taking in information about God, now we are taking it to the streets—jumping into social causes and passionately working hard to be kind people. But the internal motive can be messed up if we do all of that to simply improve the life we have in the name of Jesus. And the help we offer in Jesus' name hits a roadblock if the end game is to get people to think Jesus is nice and kind and helpful, willing and ready to improve their lives.

Improvement assumes that the core nature of the thing remains intact. If you remodel a room in your house, you pull off and replace the outer stuff—the cabinets, the fixtures, the carpet—until the job is complete, but the inner pieces remain intact. The studs in the wall, the headers above the door, and the beams in the ceiling all remain the same. The core nature is intact, but you have improved the look and feel of the place.

Jesus didn't come to remodel your life. He came to *be* your life.

My wife and I have watched our friends go through remodels of their homes. What begins with excitement over change quickly turns to stress when walls get knocked down and rooms are separated by plastic tarps. With the noise of the work, the endless coming and going of contractors, the date of completion—which keeps getting bumped back, while the price keeps going up—a home remodel is one of the most stressful things a marriage can go through.

Jesus never remodels us. He doesn't improve us. Our very natures are the issue, not the cosmetic bits of looks, behaviors, and ambitions. He goes right to the core of our nature where the dry rot has corrupted the very integrity of our lives.

Jesus didn't come to remodel your life. He came to *be*

your life. While most of us want only a simple remodel that will cover up the rotting boards, Jesus plans to *crucify* our corrupted humanity and replace it with his perfect humanity.

We can't get into the kingdom with the life we have, because the kingdom in its essence is the life of Jesus expressed through his followers, who have been crucified with Christ so they no longer live, but Christ lives in them (Galatians 2:20).

A few months ago we gathered the men in our community together and began to dream about what it could look like in our church and our community if we collectively took to following Jesus seriously. That first night you could feel the testosterone in the air. It was electric, and you couldn't tell if we needed to capture something, or kill something, or just barbeque large pieces of meat. But the sound of hundreds of men singing together about the greatness of their King was powerful.

That night we all wrote out the sins we felt were keeping us from following Christ fully. Almost everyone wrote out their particular sin, put their email and phone number on the card, and handed it in. The level of vulnerability was staggering, and I was deeply humbled that they were entrusting their ugliest places to us as leaders. In confessing what the most corrupted boards of their inner life looked like, they were not looking for new light fixtures or a coat of paint but for complete demolition and total overhaul.

For the next few months I read over the cards, thought

about the men, and prayed a lot, asking God what he wanted to do in us. The truth that stood out to me was that we were normal, sinful men, and many of us were tired. Like being fifteen years into a home remodeling job with the constant work, effort, chaos, frustration, and overall hopelessness of having no end in sight—we were tired!

A couple of weeks before we met again, my friend Rob gave me a couple of lectures from T. F. Torrance on the mediation of Christ. The focus of Torrance's teaching was how Christ mediated our relationship to the Father. Torrance explained that it was not simply our remodeled life that we offered to the Father—a remodeled life would never be sufficient. And the honest confession of the men in my community affirmed this point. No matter how hard we tried or how well we perfected our remodeling project, it would never be enough.

> **Worn out from dragging around dead bodies, we assume that whatever it takes to be a good Christian is something that eludes us. We just don't have what it takes.**

We are people carrying around our crucified bodies working very hard to resuscitate them through great theology and good works, but the end result is always the same. Our desire for God is not strong enough, our purity is not pure enough, our faith is not big enough, and our efforts are not powerful enough to create life. Worn out from dragging around dead bodies, we assume that whatever it takes to be a good Christian is something that eludes us. We just don't have what it takes.

The promise of God revealed to us in Jesus is that our attempts will never be enough. In a remarkable act of love, Jesus crucified us with himself, so that we no longer live but Christ lives in us.

As I stood before the men in my community that night, the message I shared was that they could call off the remodeling project. It was not going to work, and God never intended it to work. Christ has already given us his life. His perfect human life. He lived without sin, faithful to God and full of desire for the kingdom with such a passion that he gave up his life on a cross out of love for the Father.

The life we have been striving for is Jesus' life. It has already been lived, perfected, and given to us. We can let go of our lives, our rotted beams and sinful ways, and instead love and worship Jesus.

Jesus' desire for the Father is the desire we trust in. His faithfulness to God is what we stand in. His purity is perfect and we celebrate it because it's our own. Everything Jesus lived in his humanity is ours. We move out of the remodeling nightmare of our broken and dead life and we move into the expansive glorious life of Jesus' perfect humanity.

Jesus said whoever wants to save his life will lose it. I think this is what he meant. Our life was crucified in him two thousand years ago. In giving it up we actually no longer live, but Christ lives in us. We gain the life we have always desired, because to desire life is to desire Jesus. In him *is life*.

For the Christ follower, the kingdom of God is inside of us—the life of Jesus alive, active, pulsing with spirit and passion. The life we live in these bodies by the power of the Holy Spirit is not a remodeled life but a life of faith in Jesus' life. We can claim that which we could not gain on our own to be ours through the awe-inspiring power of Christ in us. The scraps and timbers of our remodeling attempts can be bulldozed away, because in their place Jesus has shown up, building his life in us by his power and grace.

Life. Life over death. The Creator living in and through his creatures. This is the beginning of a kingdom without end, one where the full nature of divine life is demonstrated by God's people.

The only hope the world has for an actual demonstration of the kingdom breaking into our world through the church is Jesus' life, breaking into a world of death through those who have given up their lives and trusted that Christ lives in them.

This is where the desire for life finds its fulfillment. Our life that leaks out of us and is never sufficient in this world is transformed in Jesus. Life over death is a different life. The depths of our desires can find a home in Jesus. You were created by the Creator for the life of the Creator to pulse through your very being. Jesus is the author of life and the giver of it. Let your heart put its hope in him. Let

Sell off your reduced desires, your cheap imitations, so that you can have what you most deeply want: the King of life.

your faith well up in him. This life may sound too good to be true, but it is here, in Jesus, breaking in.

The fear we feel is real. What if we put our hope down here, resting the full weight of our heart in Christ? What if we found this treasure called life buried in the unassuming field of Jesus of Nazareth and all we needed to do was to sell everything we owned to buy that field?

Do it. Sell the farm, and take your protective grip off your heart. Give up your life, so that you can gain it. Go in your joy and do what you have to do. Sell off your reduced desires, your cheap imitations, so that you can have what you most deeply want: the King of life, the King of *your* life.

Perhaps right here in the midst of all this talk about life over death, desire caught up in the crucified and resurrected King, passion pulsing through your heart—right here you are tempted to think about how foolish and utterly stupid this all sounds. Right when you feel hope rising up within you—and Jesus seems to be the King you have always wanted and hoped he would be—then your head jumps in and protests about how ridiculous this all sounds. You envision having to explain to a friend or even your spouse this large thing that is growing inside of you, and quickly you think it all sounds too crazy.

Here is what I would tell you: that is what faith feels like. You are betting your life on Jesus. You are putting everything you have on Jesus being life, Jesus overcoming death, Jesus bringing a kingdom that puts the world back together. We have to come to this place if faith is going to move us into the kingdom called desire. The revolution that is happening is coming through those who are foolish and ridiculous and dumb enough to have the courage to sell everything they can't hold onto, to gain a life they can never lose. What seems foolish in this world makes total sense in the kingdom.

The world is made beautiful by those who are willing to trust Jesus in such a way that they risk offending the consensus of the masses by imagining a world that doesn't now exist. It is made beautiful by those willing to believe Jesus is the King of life, that life breaks into the midst of death, faith shows up in the middle of unbelief, and courage can appear in the midst of fear. This community of Jesus people is becoming a people who live lives of ridiculous risk because their hearts have been captured by something this world cannot contain or destroy.

This takes us back to our fear of death. Going back to the canyon and looking across to the risen King, and then staring down at the vile creature that seeks to kill and destroy, I realize that until I love Jesus more than this world, I will never experience the life that overcomes death. But when I embrace Jesus' life as my life, then I see that I have already died in him and been raised in him. I no longer fear death. Jesus has saved me.

The King of life reigns. Jesus Christ lives. People are living with unshackled imagination into the true, the good, and the beautiful. People are risking death because they believe they have a life that can't be put out. Bet your heart on it. Risk your desire on him.

Buy the field with joy. He is the treasure you cannot lose.

FORMATION QUESTIONS

1. In what ways do you think you have just wanted Jesus to remodel your life as opposed to completely remaking you?
2. What has disappointed you about your life?
3. If Jesus' life is the life we trust in, what relief does that bring to you?
4. What prevents you from putting your hope in Jesus to be your life?
5. Is this life enough for you right now, or are you finding in yourself a desire for something that this world will not satisfy, as C. S. Lewis talked about?
6. How would you describe your desire for life?

SIX

Jesus, the Object of Desire

People are attracted to the kingdom of God because the world desperately needs help. In our world, genocide is alive and well, human trafficking is rampant, and natural disasters devastate the world's poorest countries. Millions of people have no access to clean drinking water and bury their children from something as simple as diarrhea. These are just a few of the glaring issues that keep our world in a constant state of brokenness and need. On top of all of this, millions of people still have not heard the gospel of Jesus Christ and are living lives bound up in the kingdom of darkness, where sin is holding them captive in an unmerciful grip.

On a more personal level, *we* desperately need help. Our marriages need mending, our parenting needs direction, our battles against anger or porn or addiction or sloth need to be waged and won.

The idea of a kingdom where beauty and truth, love and

grace, break in and reign amidst these devastating issues and debilitating personal problems is something we all long for. To see it, taste it, and be part of it is nothing short of extraordinary. We want more of it. When we get our hands dirty and our hearts broken in service of the kingdom, we are left longing for and wanting more. More justice, more mercy, more love, more hope, more salvation.

But there is a subtle danger in all of this. When we desire the kingdom, we have to be sure not to miss the King. Living in a world where government is working far away in some state capital or farther away in Washington, D.C., we may feel its effects but have little or no contact with the leaders who make the decisions. We are disconnected from the political authority governing our personal worlds, which may lead us to feel disconnected to the spiritual authority that governs our lives.

Since we experience a culture where we have little relationship to our leaders, we can easily assume the same is true of the kingdom of God. We get to live within the context of the kingdom, serving and working to see it displayed in the midst of our world, but still have little or no meaningful experience of the King himself. The longing for life that we don't possess and cannot gain from this world will remain until we find fulfillment in the King himself.

We were not made to do the supernatural work of redemptive love in our own strength. In fact it is impossible to do it.

The fresh awakening of kingdom language and activity within the church is incredibly promising. We dream of a church that no longer creates dividing lines between ourselves and the world around us, but lovingly and courageously jumps into the mess of our world, giving herself away for the lives of other people.

But danger lurks when we desire the kingdom but have no meaningful experience of the King. We were not made to do the supernatural work of redemptive love in our own strength. In fact it is impossible to do it. Jesus said that apart from him, we can do nothing. So we must remain in him — because only then do we bear much fruit, fruit that will last. To go into this broken world disconnected from the King is to reduce the kingdom to some type of activism or church program with no ultimate or redemptive end.

Not only do we get disconnected from the King; we also get disconnected from each other. One camp decides it loves to serve and work for justice, but it can't stand evangelism. And when they hear the word *evangelism*, they write off those who are still doing it or are talking about it. *Haven't they heard we aren't doing that anymore? We love them without words.*

Meanwhile, another camp loves evangelism. They love sharing their faith, talking about Jesus, and seeing people come to faith, and when they see people working with the poor or marginalized they wonder if they are liberal and quickly become suspicious of their doctrine.

These tensions between the two camps cause polarization in God's church, among God's people. Neo-liberals and neo-fundamentalists abound, quick to pigeonhole each other: who's right, who's wrong, who's inspired, who's dangerous?

Which camp is Jesus in? That's the question. Because everyone is claiming he is on their side. But Jesus isn't in one camp or another; he is at work in the tension of holding together the proclamation of the gospel embodied in a people who lovingly serve the world. The choice is not *either* evangelism *or* social action but both/and.

Jesus lived and announced the good news through a life of sacrificial compassion that ended on a cross of substitution, culminating in a resurrection that would qualify him to create one new humanity in him by faith in his blood. And where Jesus is doing his saving, forgiving, resurrecting, healing, redeeming, serving work through the lives of those whom he indwells by his Spirit, there the kingdom of light is breaking into the kingdom of darkness. There the reign of the King is showing up within his people and through his people.

The choice is not *either* evangelism *or* social action but both/and.

He shows up when a group of people work together on a new translation of the Bible, applying academic rigor to their sacred task.

He shows up when a group of volunteers converge on a disaster site, bringing food, medical supplies, shelter, and comfort to the victims.

He shows up in the intimate actions and daily ministrations of the believing mother and father, who nurture their children in and through his love.

He shows up in the board room of a powerful multi-national company, where a CEO uses his business acumen to create and maintain jobs, to build wealth for shareholders, and to create an environment where employees can thrive and there's a bigger bottom line than money.

He shows up on the streets of the city, where believers reach out to the homeless, the addicted, the prostitute, and the pimp.

I am not sure Jesus would understand our polarizing taxonomies. Is there any place where Jesus' kingdom cannot show up? If Jesus himself hung out with prostitutes and political leaders, religious folk and outcasts, the wealthy and the working class, the sick and the crazy, the old and the young — is there any place he cannot go?

We don't get the kingdom without the King, and if we find ourselves in Jesus then we can trust him to overflow his love and life into the world and display the kingdom through us. Not either/or, not this camp or that camp, but both/and.

Two different stories come to my mind. One was a guy I know who was preparing to be a pastor. We talked about Jesus and his kingdom and were considering Jesus' call to go into that world and be light in darkness, to eat with the contemporary tax collectors and sinners — essentially, the people who were not going to be in a rush to get up on Sunday morning and run off to church.

For the first few weeks the conversation was philosophical. We enjoyed bantering around the ideas that Scripture presented to us about the kingdom of God. But as the days went on it was becoming apparent that we were not just talking about ideas, but getting our own hearts and lives into this path Jesus was calling his people to follow.

Ideas turned into actual places in the community with great need, where darkness prevailed, and statistics became actual names and faces of people who were living in the turmoil of oppression, addiction, and poverty. His questions began to fade and the conversation became a lot more serious. Finally one day he got very honest.

"I don't want to get polluted by them." He said it quietly and humbly.

At first I didn't know exactly what he meant, but it quickly became clear. His honesty was beautiful, but the truth was not. That's how it always is when we come clean, I suppose.

He feared that his faith would somehow be corrupted by people whose lifestyles he thought were morally inferior. His doctrines may have been intact, the things he understood about God remained certain, but his experience of Jesus failed to move him into the heart of Jesus. He was afraid of the others.

The irony of course is that in his theology he could get all the answers right on the deity of Christ, the doctrine of atonement, salvation by faith, even the necessity to go into all the world and make disciples. But when the Holy Spirit brought him face-to-face with real places that Jesus wanted to take him and real people Jesus wanted to love through him, he punted.

The other person is a guy who had the utmost passion for social issues. From concern for the environment to love of the poor, he carried a zeal that was unmatched. He worked tirelessly for several causes—all of which were really good things that carried the possibility of bringing about real social change in our community.

By any estimation, you would believe that he was sold out to Jesus and was living out a radical faith. He lived frugally, shopped locally, biked everywhere, and never backed down from confronting people who were apathetic to the plight of the world. Then one day he disappeared. I hadn't seen him for several weeks and began asking around.

It turned out he was walking away from Jesus. A crisis in his life had left him doubting that God was real, and he was burned out and tired. The causes that drew him into passionate service didn't fade, like you might think. Despite his lack of faith, and despite his burnout, he remained extremely zealous for those causes, only they are no longer tied to any redemptive hope in Christ.

The first guy worshiped his religious security (and perhaps even his superiority). The second guy worshiped the cause and the social agenda. One chose the kingdom of the church and the other the kingdom of the culture.

Two stories of two very different people. One runs from Jesus by going back inside the church and separating himself from culture, and the other runs from Jesus by throwing himself into causes for social change. The constant is that they are both running away from the heart of Christ.

At the core, this is a worship issue. The first guy worshiped his religious security (and perhaps even his superiority). The second guy worshiped the cause and the social agenda. One chose the kingdom of the church and the other the kingdom of the culture.

Perhaps that's too simplistic, but we see the point. In both cases, each person was in the midst of something they desired, believing Jesus was on their side. But in the end neither was truly interested in Jesus as much as they were their personal passions and preferences. Each one was certain they were participating in the life of the kingdom, and maybe in some way they were or are, but we are only guessing on that. The only way we can be certain we are participating in the life of the kingdom is when we do what we do out of a desire for Jesus.

Christ's love will compel us to love the other, and Christ's beauty and excellence will ensure we won't turn a good work into an idol. This only happens as we apprehend a vision of the living Christ that is more attractive than our personal protection and more excellent than fixing the social issues of our day.

In the kingdom of God, Christ is the King *and* the cause, but we cannot grasp this idea on our own. We need the Holy Spirit to reveal this vision of Jesus to us through the Scriptures, so that by grace our hearts can grab onto it in faith.

The King who healed the sick and raised the dead and continues to do his redeeming work in our lives as the resurrected conqueror of sin and death invites us to drink in his untamed and holy love. As we begin to grasp this by faith, our core doctrines move from the page and into real life. Our church agendas or social issues

We leave the polarizing place of choosing between church or culture when Jesus becomes the object of our desire.

must *never* usurp the relationship that resides at the center of our spiritual lives, which is Christ in us, the hope of glory.

To not live in the present experience of Jesus *in us* and *with us* is to retreat from his holy love, reduce his saving passion, and remove us from the very places and people whom he has come to rescue. The world that you want — full of justice, love, beauty, and truth — is the world he is creating in his people and through his people. A kingdom defined by a passionate new humanity who live out of the depths of the King's love.

We leave the polarizing place of choosing between church or culture when Jesus becomes the object of our desire. We have to. To desire Jesus is to live into his reign and display his love to the world wherever he calls us, whether that be church or board room, the home or the streets, the neighborhood or the mission field. To do justice and love mercy in its fullest sense is most authentic and Christ honoring when we have received mercy and been justified by a gracious King.

FORMATION QUESTIONS

1. Think about the story of the two guys who were avoiding Jesus: one avoiding him by hiding in the kingdom of the church, and one by hiding in the kingdom of the world. Which kingdom do you tend to run toward to hide from Jesus?

2. Do you think there is a difference between worshiping the King and serving the kingdom, or would you see them as one and the same?

3. In the kingdom, Christ is the King and the cause. How does that affect how we serve others in the world?

4. What are you currently doing for Jesus, and how does that display his kingdom on this earth?

SEVEN

The Love of God

I fell in love with my wife when I was nineteen. It's one of those stories that people roll their eyes when I talk about it because it was one of those love-at-first-sight stories. I saw her in a large classroom in Bradley Hall. We looked at each other across the room, and I knew I was going to marry her. Over the next few months that initial sensation would grow and deepen as we spent more time together, then got engaged, and finally married about six months later.

Our love for each other has deepened over the years but also has been stretched. We have admitted to each other several times that we are selfish at the core, and there have been several hard seasons where we remained committed to our marriage but found it hard to be selfless and love each other the way we knew God had called us to. We still really love each other all these years later, but we both realize that the unconditional and selfless love that we need to give each other oftentimes isn't in us. We need a love that we don't possess in order to love each other in a way that is worthy of our marriage.

The apostle John writes simply and profoundly in 1 John that God *is* love. Love is not simply something that God does; it is more than that. It is definitional to his being God. The essence of God's love is most vividly displayed within himself. Love is the bond between Father, Son, and Spirit in the being of the triune God.

Love — perfect and in its purest form — is part of the central core of God. Love is not God. God is more than love, but he is not less than love. God *is* love.

God expresses love most perfectly in a dynamic relationship within the Godhead between the persons of the Trinity. The Father loving the Son and the Son loving the Father, the Spirit dynamically expressing this love between the two, and everyone always glorifying one another — perfect love expressed in complete harmony, perfect communion.

Such perfect love is easier to define on paper than to get into our hearts. The idea of perfect love expressed in absolute relationship is foreign to us. We think of the best love we have ever experienced — between a parent and a child, a husband and a wife, a girlfriend and a boyfriend. The moments we've shared with loved ones are so perfect we want to stop time, so that we can experience the full weight and joy of love. But we can't. Time keeps moving. The moments are simply moments.

God expresses love most perfectly in a dynamic relationship within the Godhead between the persons of the Trinity.

Love also runs deeper than just moments. The depth of love between a child and her parents can grow and thrive for years and years until the mother is in her nineties and the daughter in her seventies, and still that bond of love is deep and strong. Friends can go deeper and deeper in relationship as the years go by. They travel together through more pain, more joy, more life, and the sum of those years wraps around them like a cord that grows stronger with each passing year, another strand of life and of friendship.

Love can grow deep. I believe underneath all our other desires we have a desire for perfected love, which is a desire for God because God is love. You may have to pull back the layers, but it is there. If our desires tend to lead to disappointment as we have seen, perhaps our hearts were made for something greater than earth can offer. We were made to live in a kingdom of perfected love where we love and are loved by Jesus.

If beneath all other desires we find the desire for perfected love and God *is* perfect love, then our ultimate desire is for God, since he is both beyond what the world can offer and the very definition of love. His kingdom breaks into our very desires with heavenly love reigning in our hearts through Jesus our King.

The problem is we are often crippled in our deepest places, where love is desperately needed but only arrives for a moment. We can hear about love growing deeper in relationships of friends and family, but we have to admit we have many relationships where love doesn't grow at all. Our desire for love can be strong, but strong desire doesn't create the thing that we desire. We have to admit that desire is not the creator or sustainer of love. Desire is simply the place where our longing for love shows up.

Perhaps that is all desire is, just a longing. But it is an important longing. We want to be loved, meaningfully and personally, and we want another to love. We want love to grow, to go the distance, to become and keep becoming.

We have to admit that desire is not the creator or sustainer of love. Desire is simply the place where our longing for love shows up.

God *is* love.

Which is compelling, but as long as it remains just an idea or proposition, it can never become more than that, which is why God moved into the drama of creating the world.

God didn't need to create the world; he is sustained eternally in complete and pure love simply by being who he is. He is satisfied in his own love, finds ultimate joy in it, and is deeply related in his own person because he is a being in a community of love.

But he did create the world. Creation itself was an act of love.

God created the world—you and me, all of history, oak trees and geese, cattle, flowers, weather—as an act of love. But we don't always see it as an act of love. We sometimes sit in the midst of our broken world and wonder why he created it at all. But God desired that his creation would be brought into his communion of love simply to enjoy him and be united with him forever.

In this union we find something extraordinary. In a very real sense the Father, Son, and Spirit created the world to gain a bride for the Son out of his created people. God desired to extend his love beyond himself and into his creation. He did this by redeeming fallen creation so he could bring us into perfect union with Jesus.

As the creation story unfolds it's not hard to think that the whole thing got out of control. The God who is love (full of good intentions) speaks creation into place, and then angels fall, his first people rebel against him, creation goes into a tailspin, death arrives, humanity turns in on itself . . . and soon violence, rape, murder, greed, natural disasters, and self-centered people are making enemies of each other and God, corrupting the whole plan of creation. It makes you sit back and wonder why he created it in the first place. This is an important question, because the answer we discover is critical to understanding the nature of God's love as it is expressed in his intention for creation.

God intervenes in the lives of sinful and rebellious humanity and continues to create the possibility of relationship with himself, even though humanity has become a train wreck.

God intervenes in the lives of sinful and rebellious humanity and continues to create the possibility of relationship with himself, even though humanity has become a train wreck.

The drama continues to unfold beyond the garden of Eden.

God chooses Abraham and creates a nation out of the miracle of Isaac.

He calls Moses and gives that nation the law so they can live into the love of God, but they keep blowing it.

He rescues them from Egypt and leads them into the Promised Land, but they worship other gods.

He sends prophets to remind them they have sinned and need to repent, but they keep sinning.

Finally he sends his Son ... whom they reject and kill.

Here in the middle of the story, the Son of God becomes flesh, God and humanity united in the person of Jesus. He dies for our sins, so we can be forgiven and accepted by the Father. The Holy Spirit is sent to give us new life because our old life was dead, but we continue to struggle because we still live in fallen bodies that one day will die. But thanks be to God, we will receive new bodies in heaven, where we will once again live in perfection just as Adam did in the garden of Eden.

If this is all we see in the story, then we are missing a key aspect of the love of God. With this limited view, we will soon find ourselves back in Genesis 2, only in heaven and not on earth.

God's love accomplished something much bigger through his redeeming story. If we stop here we really cannot adequately answer the question of why God created the universe, particularly if it was an act of love. If being restored to Adam's sinless state is all that we are promised, then there is a good chance when we get to heaven there will be another fall. Adam and Eve had unfallen bodies, sinless wills. They were perfectly free, and they chose autonomy over relationship, love of self over love of God. If all we are restored to in heaven is a return to Eden, then we are in trouble. Even the glory of Eden is still not enough.

The God who is love created the world as an act of love for something so amazing that it's difficult to get our minds around it. Not only did he create, pursue, redeem, justify, sanctify, and glorify people who were dead in their sins, but he did it so the Son could have a bride. You are the bride. The whole drama of creation, covenant, and kingdom points to this critical and often missed theme that is central to the purpose of creation.

Love risks.

Risk is why we often find love painful. When we love we give ourselves wholly to something or someone, which creates security in us if the one whom we love receives us in fidelity. Yet many things interfere with love, from tragedy, to pain, to loss, to infidelity. To love is to risk all of those things.

What seems unfathomable to us is that God would take such a risk. We can't imagine that God would allow himself to be subject to the possibility of rejection or infidelity, but that is exactly what he did.

In creating the world as an act of love and passionately loving those whom he created, God took a risk that would ultimately leave him incarnated in full humanity and hanging on the cross. He didn't do this only to justify his original creation that he couldn't quite keep from falling apart. Not at all.

God is not fixing the world by redeeming the fall, but

is creating something that could not happen apart from the fall: uniting us to himself in Jesus, the one who is God and man.

He risked creation and the fall of humanity which he knew full well was coming, because through the fall of free-willed humanity, he could enact a salvation whereby he himself would become human in Jesus, die in our place on the cross, conquer sin and death, rise from the dead through resurrection, bring about a new creation that will never perish like the old creation, and *then* — and this is a big *then* — unite himself to those whom he saves by his Spirit.

God created the world and allowed the fall, because through Jesus' redemption a deeper relationship of love could be created — a better love than Adam experienced walking in the garden with God.

God created the world and allowed the fall, because through Jesus' redemption a deeper relationship of love could be created — a better love than Adam experienced walking in the garden with God. Something *better* than unfallen Adam was created in Jesus. We are brought into the love of the Father for the Son, and by the Son.

Those who find themselves in Jesus are united with the Father through the Son by the Spirit. We are brought into the communion of perfect love because the person of the beloved Son lives within us and we within him. The kingdom shows up in Jesus, and Jesus is alive within us. In this union with Christ desires are redeemed and fulfilled because this is our love story. We are the one that the Son has brought home to the Father.

We can now partake of his divine nature (2 Peter 1:4) and are brought into the divine love of the Father, Son, and Spirit, thus making us the bride of Christ. This is why creation is an act of love, because the point of creation is to draw God's image-bearing people into his eternal communion of love not simply with us or around us but *in* us, transforming our nature as we find ourselves in Christ.

This *is* love. United in Christ.

Through the drama of creation and redemption, God used the fall as the very vehicle through which his redemption could come and needed to come, so that he could create something more than original creation. Jesus brings about a *new* creation defined by our union with Christ through the Spirit. This does not make us divine in our own nature, but allows us to participate in Jesus' nature through the mystical union of us and Christ.

This union assures that we will never be separated from Christ.

This is the love story of being united with Christ and participating in his life.

This has been the stance of many of our most significant church fathers from Augustine to Luther and Calvin.

Calvin put it this way:

I acknowledge that we are devoid of this incomparable gift until Christ becomes ours. Therefore, to that union of the head and members, the residence of Christ in our hearts, in fine, the mystical union, we assign the highest rank, Christ when he becomes ours making us partner with him in the gifts with which he was endued. Hence we do not view him as at a distance and without us, but as we have put him on, and been ingrafted into his body, he deigns to make us one with himself, and, therefore, we glory in having a fellowship of righteousness with him.[3]

Calvin understood the love of Jesus expressed in the saving act of bringing us into a union of love. He grasped the powerful reality that Christ in all of his glory is ours in this mystical union. The one who is love has united us to himself so that we are grafted into his life: one with God, who is love; brought into communion with the Father in union with the Son by the indwelling of the Spirit. And this weighty truth expresses itself in the daily experience of Christ in us.

Desire begins to find its fulfillment in the person of Jesus because in Christ the love of the Father is given to us.

Jesus leads us to the Father, who accepts and welcomes us because we are in Christ. Creation is an act of love, because through creation the Father secured us for his Son. The Son entered creation through the womb of Mary, taking

---

3. John Calvin, *Institutes of the Christian Religion*, 3.11.10.

on actual humanity to die a passionate death for the one he loves, which is you.

This is the essence of our salvation. Scripture continues to testify to the reality that we are united with Christ.

> This is love: not that we loved God, but that he loved us and sent his Son as an atoning sacrifice for our sins. (1 John 4:10)
>
> God demonstrates his own love for us in this: While we were still sinners, Christ died for us. (Romans 5:8)
>
> God has poured out his love into our hearts by the Holy Spirit, whom he has given us. (Romans 5:5)
>
> Who shall separate us from the love of Christ? . . . [Nothing] in all creation, will be able to separate us from the love of God that is in Christ Jesus our Lord. (Romans 8:35, 39)
>
> The Spirit of truth . . . abides with you and will be in you. (John 14:17 NASB)
>
> In that day you will know that I am in My Father, and you in Me, and I in you. (John 14:20 NASB)
>
> To them God chose to make known how great among the Gentiles are the riches of the glory of this mystery, which is Christ in you, the hope of glory. (Colossians 1:27 ESV)
>
> "For this reason a man will leave his father and mother and be united to his wife, and the two will become one flesh." This is a profound mystery —

but I am talking about Christ and the church. (Ephesians 5:31–32)

Jesus becomes the object of our desire when we develop a vision of him that attracts us to him and draws us away from lesser loves. In union with Jesus our desire for love finds the ultimate fulfillment — not a moment of love that we must collect and then hold on to while we wait for the next one, but an eternity united with the one who *is* love.

Jesus becomes the object of our desire when we develop a vision of him that attracts us to him and draws us away from lesser loves.

This love will not disappoint us, because the eternal communion of love between Father, Son, and Spirit brings us fully into the love of God.

This love compels us to respond. We don't initiate love toward God; we receive it in Jesus and as Jesus. The creation drama is the most passionate love story ever told, and God is the pursuing lover. We are invited to respond to love that so furiously and recklessly has come after us in Christ.

The definition of grace that seems most appropriate to me is simply: *God's love given to us in Jesus and as Jesus.* This is a story of grace. God's love is ours in Christ.

God's love is all the more attractive in this light. It is different than we imagine or experience in our memories of love, but true and present — demonstrated for us on the cross, secured eternally by the empty tomb, and poured out into our hearts by the Holy Spirit.

Creation is an act of love. The Father creates a bride for the Son, the Son takes on our createdness to redeem us, and the Spirit is poured out into our hearts, uniting us to the Son forever. Where we see the Father love the Son or the Son love the Father, there we are in him, and this love is personally applied to our hearts by his Spirit.

In his kingdom, love is the primary quality of relationship, and the quality of that love is secured by the love of God. It is the love of God that flows to the people of the kingdom and travels through the people of the kingdom, to each other and the world around them.

When I realize that I am united with Christ by *his* work and *his* choice then I can rest.

If this is true then we have to confess that this is our story. All the other narratives that we may have told ourselves are not the true story. When I realize that I am united with Christ by *his* work and *his* choice then I can rest. I don't have to create another story or a better story, because I have been brought into *the* story.

I am loved by Jesus and in Jesus.

You are loved by Jesus and in Jesus.

This relationship changes all other relationships. I am no longer united to sin and death because I have been united to Jesus.

I am no longer united to the American dream story that declares I am what I make myself.

I am no longer united to the need to clamor after people's approval.

This love is enough, and it frees me up to serve others instead of using others.

This is love. This is what our hearts long for. Let your desire rest in him.

FORMATION QUESTIONS

1. Why is creation an act of love?
2. What does it mean to be united with Christ?
3. How does being united with Christ impact your definition of relationship with God?
4. God's love was given to us *in* Jesus and *as* Jesus. Does that make his love depersonalized to you or more personal? Explain.
5. In what ways does the highly relational picture of union with Christ change how you think of your faith?

EIGHT

Responding to the King

In light of the profound demonstration of love discussed in the last chapter, we have to ask the implicit question: Why would God love *us*? You can probably think of better candidates for God to pursue. Our standards of value have been shaped by a world hell-bent on the survival of the fittest. We are trained at an early age that there is a certain look, a certain body type, a certain IQ, a certain set of skills, a certain family background, a certain moral pedigree that is required for anyone to be worthy of notice.

God's love is his nature and he is so full of mercy that he has not chosen whom he loves based on their personal achievements or perceived worth. His love is given to those who are *not* worthy. He is not seeking to unite himself only to those who meet certain qualifications of looks, personality, and aptitude, but instead he has chosen a bride who was once an orphaned whore.

You heard me right. *We* are the orphaned whores.

That image may offend you, but we see this theme play

out throughout the Old Testament, especially in Ezekiel 16, which paints a graphic picture of a child rejected at birth, kicking around in her own blood, who is rescued, brought up properly, develops into a beautiful young woman — and promptly becomes a whore. The image is harsh, but we are both of those: orphaned and whores. We are desperate and needy without God. We are unfaithful and easily persuaded to love a myriad of things other than God. That is what makes grace all the more attractive. Grace: God's love for us, the orphaned whore whom he makes his bride.

Our love differs from the love of God because our love is polluted with the love of self over and above God. We pursue lesser things, desire lesser things, and love lesser things because we ultimately love ourselves and not God.

Sin therefore is not so much the absence of moral good but the presence of self-love over love for God. Love for God can lead us to change our behaviors, but simply having right behavior does not mean we are behaving well because we love God. In fact, we may be acting a certain way that appears to look very good, but the truth is we are doing it because we are proud of our own righteousness or want other people to think we are righteous. All of this is self-love, not love for God.

We pursue lesser things, desire lesser things, and love lesser things because we ultimately love ourselves and not God.

So we return to that question of *how*, which I deconstructed in the first chapter. How do we respond to this love that God has displayed? And especially, how can we respond given our propensity to self-love?

If you catch a glimpse of the goodness of God through the love of Christ, your desires turn. They turn away from self and toward God. This faith wells up within the heart and is motivated to respond to gracious love. The turning is in our attraction. When we are captured by the love of God, knowing we don't deserve it but we are desired by God, something happens. We find ourselves wanting Jesus, desiring Jesus, and seeking Jesus. Our response is secondary to his ultimate actions of love. Our emotions and our intellect get caught up in the love of God when we truly apprehend the radical vision of God's grace towards us — when we recognize that though we may be the orphaned whore, we are still the beloved of God.

It is hard to receive the love of God when you realize that you can never earn it, when we realize we don't have the resources to sustain the devotion that such a love is worthy of. No amount of activity that we can accomplish will be a sufficient response to this holy love. The problem shows up when we drift from chasing Christ out of attraction and desire and attempt to show Christ that we are worthy of the love of God. We do this in a thousand different ways, from serving the poor to studying theology — all of which are good, as I have said before. But they are insufficient if we trust in them to show God our devotion is worthy of his love or if we believe we have to do them to keep him loving us.

Here is where we find our desire too weak, our devotion too sporadic, our service often self-centered, our theology becoming a tool that fuels our ego. Instead of acting as the beloved people of God responding in grace through Jesus, we try through our own power to create a response that is worthy of his love. Instead of worshiping the King through our kingdom efforts, we become paid workers going through the motions.

No amount of activity that we can accomplish will be a sufficient response to this holy love.

Spirituality begins to feel like we are on a treadmill that keeps going and continues to speed up.

If I can just get over that one sin I'll be there. Then we speed up again.

If only I got busy doing something good for the King and the kingdom, I could respond sufficiently. This time the incline rises.

If I studied more and prayed more I could experience this love in a powerful way. Now we are at a full jog.

How about I leave my church and go to another church that seems to be doing things effectively in the community? That must be the missing link. Now we are running, almost sprinting.

If I shared the gospel with more people and prayed for my neighbors every day, then God would see me as worthy of his love. The sweat is pouring down, and we have to hold the sidebars just to keep from falling.

The treadmill keeps going, and we keep running, and

soon this amazing love we see displayed in Jesus feels like a setup. We want it, he offered it, but we can't seem to find a path of devotion worthy of it. Tired, some will keep running, but others will find something easier to wrap their desire around. They'll get off the treadmill and walk away from it all.

We stand before this impossibly beautiful love, the amazing reality that we are united to this love in Christ, and then we admit that we don't have the resources within ourselves to apply it or capture it. Our desire is too weak, our devotion too small, our resources too limited, and at every corner where sin has found us we are reminded we are unfaithful.

Jesus understands this weakness. The incarnation of Christ allows us to come to the Father and become participants in God's perfect love, not based on our desire, devotion, or resources, but on Christ's.

Jesus is the divine Son who became a man. He is not half God, half man, but fully and uniquely one person existing as both God and man. As God, he can communicate the love and goodness of the Father to us with precision and exactness. Hebrews 1 tells us that Jesus is the radiance of God's glory and the exact representation of his being. If we want to know what God is like, we look at Jesus. He reveals God to us.

But Jesus is also fully human, and as a man Jesus lived a life of perfect devotion. He accomplished what we will never accomplish. He always did the will of the Father; he was tempted in every way but was without sin. He prayed enough, was compassionate enough, was merciful enough, loved enough, served enough, was humble enough, and worshiped the Father with complete love and faithfulness. Jesus' humanity was not only the way in which the Father was revealed to humanity but was also the way in which humanity responded in complete devotion to the Father. He succeeded where Israel had failed and where you and I fail every day.

He accomplished it. Jesus is humanity's perfect response to the love of God.

As T. F. Torrance says in his lecture on the mediation of Christ,[4] Jesus bent the heart of humanity back to the Father through his own complete and faithful human devotion. Now it is *his* life that you trust in to be your life's response to God. His devotion is enough, his faithfulness is flawless, his purity is absolute, and his worship is undivided. It is not up to you to respond in a way compatible with the magnitude of God's love. Jesus did that. He is the demonstration of God's love and the response to God's love. And you come to the Father through Jesus and in Jesus. His devotion is your devotion, his worship is your worship, his faithful-

While we are sprinting on our treadmills, trying to keep up with the love of God through an appropriate response, Jesus comes along and pulls the plug out of the wall.

---

4. Lecture given in 1973 at Regent College, Vancouver, British Columbia.

ness is your faithfulness. If we actually get that, then we desire Jesus, because Jesus is the only object truly worthy of our desire. Jesus makes peace with God for us by perfecting our response to the love of God toward us. Just be loved and enjoy God.

While we are sprinting on our treadmills, trying to keep up with the love of God through an appropriate response, Jesus comes along and pulls the plug out of the wall.

It is finished. He accomplished it.

Jesus is far more than we could hope him to be. He affirms in us that God is as good as you could ever hope for him to be. When we grasp this with the eyes of our hearts, we enthrone Jesus in our hearts as King. We don't *try* to enthrone him there; we can't *help* but enthrone him. He is our King, worthy of our worship and faith, which moves us to put the full weight of our trust in him and on him.

Christ is the only life we have to offer to God — Christ, in all of his glory, the one mediator between God and man. Now we can enter into the rest, peace, and joy of the communion of love between the Father and Son, who lives in us by his Spirit. When the heart captures this vision of Jesus, desire is transformed. Desire for Jesus is the chief desire, beside which all other desires fade.

Grace as the love of God toward us, made real to us in Jesus, is beyond what we can think to ask for. Here grace is capitalized and multifaceted as the love of God towards us. This is grace that Jesus accomplished through his perfect obedience to the Father. He obeyed for us, so that we can come to him with all that we lack, and in Christ it is enough. His perfect devotion is our perfected devotion. We trust in the perfect obedience and devotion of Jesus.

Desire for Jesus is the chief desire, beside which all other desires fade.

Embracing our smallness before the infinite love of God, we recognize that Christ is a massive sea and I am a small speck caught up in it—carried forth by it and consumed by it, yet still intact. This ocean of love is all I can see in every direction, stretching out to the horizon. Yet the seas never toss nor threaten, but simply carry me along to new places, next adventures. Christ's love is never reduced to a trickle. It is always expanding within me, because I am taking in more and more of him. And, in him, the love of God is without end.

The desire for God that I am depending on with the full weight of my trust is Jesus' desire for the Father. When Jesus' devotion is enough, and I am united in him, then my small acts of worship are combined with Jesus' perfect acts of worship, and my response of love for the Father is united with Jesus' infinite and perfect love for the Father. I'm okay in this mighty ocean because I am one with Jesus. My small, frail, and partial desire turns toward Jesus. I am captured and present, available and paying attention. This desire too will fail at times, waning in and out, but Jesus won't, so I am trusting in Jesus, not myself.

We are no longer the orphaned whore. Instead we are being made into the image of Christ, and he is our devotion. We respond to the love of God by trusting in Jesus' response to the love of the Father. We get to add our bits and pieces, and in him they are enough.

FORMATION QUESTIONS

1. If sin is defined as the presence of self-love rather than the absence of moral good, do you think you are better off or worse off?
2. In what ways does your love of self express itself?
3. Since Jesus in his human life lived out the perfect life of devotion and we simply trust in the life he lived, what freedom does that bring to your faith?
4. In what ways do you find yourself running on the treadmill of trying to respond to the love of God?
5. In what ways does trusting in Jesus' life as your response to the Father bring you hope?
6. How is this different than the way you would normally think about responding to the love of God?
7. Does this make you desire Jesus more or less? Explain.

NINE

The Security That Gives Birth to Hope

Like many Christians I know, one of my deepest, most persistent fears is that my faith is insufficient. Despite the deep truth of the gospel that proclaims the love of God to me in Jesus, I can't quite experience all that is good in the gospel. And I think I can't experience it because my faith is not strong enough.

It goes something like this: God reveals how attractive his love is and I set out to believe it. I may read more, or pray more, or journal about the changes that Jesus' love makes in my life. Then something happens. Some trigger goes off inside of me and I drift. It may be something as simple as busyness, where a hectic week leaves me with little time for being silent and alone with God. Almost without notice I drift into a place where I am quick to rely on myself rather than Jesus. After a few days or weeks of this I am empty. I'm not experiencing God's love, I am vulnerable to doubt, and I end up trying to justify myself through my own abilities.

When I find space to pay attention to my heart I can realize where I am and turn back to the love of God. But honestly, after going through years of doing this, drifting in and drifting out, I come to the conclusion that my faith is insufficient. Here is my dilemma: everything I desire is in Jesus, but I can't access him because my faith is too weak or inconsistent. What hope do I have?

If faith comes from God, did he not give me enough? If I am saved by faith then I have to work hard at believing, but what if I can't make faith happen? What security do I have?

Before I know it faith becomes a work and no longer resembles a gift of grace. I am working at making faith happen so that I can receive grace, and now everything is backwards. Hope disappears and desire fades to black. If the only assurance I have is my ability to believe, then I must conclude that I don't have much assurance at all. Jesus is holding out the gift of life and I stand before him with amputated limbs trying to grasp something that I don't have the hands to grab onto.

What makes the good news really great is that my assurance of faith doesn't rest on my faith. My assurance of faith rests in Jesus alone.

What makes the good news really great is that my assurance of faith doesn't rest on my faith. My assurance of faith rests in Jesus alone. We need something larger than our experience or our own reality to secure our heart's desire.

We are not called to trust in our faith. We are invited to trust in Jesus. In the incarnation Jesus became our new humanity, which means that we were represented in Jesus as he lived the perfect human life in relationship to the Father. He had perfect faith to trust the Father in every situation, even on the night of his betrayal when he faced immanent crucifixion. He obeyed God, perfectly fulfilling the law of God in every situation. He loved other people perfectly and revealed the Father's heart to the world in how he related to people. Jesus had perfect faith, and trust, and love, and mercy. Jesus fulfilled the human requirements of a faithful life, a life of faith that you and I simply can't do on our own. So we don't have to trust in our ability to make faith happen — we trust Jesus. We put the focus of our faith in Jesus, the perfect human and the Word made flesh.

Jesus fulfilled the human requirements of a faithful life, a life of faith that you and I simply can't do on our own.

In trusting Jesus I trust a living person. I am not trusting in an act that took place two thousand years ago on the cross, but I am trusting the one who accomplished that act of salvation on the cross and rose from the dead, ascended into heaven, and is *alive* today.

The fact that Jesus is alive today makes all the difference. Scripture tells us that because Christ ascended he could send his Holy Spirit into the world for us. Through the Holy Spirit Jesus stays with us until the end. The Holy Spirit also gives us our faith. He reveals the Father to our hearts in the person of the Son, and he invites us to participate in Jesus' life.

When I am faced with the insufficiency of my faith, I normally am focusing on something that I lack. The truth is we all lack what we need to be the people that God asks us to be. If it is up to us then we are without hope. If we are left to strive to be what we can never be, that impossible battle will kill desire and take away all assurance I have that God is going to accept me.

The New Testament, instead, paints a picture of participation between us and Christ. The living Christ is alive in me through the Spirit. I don't make him show up by faith; I have faith that he is showing up. The subtle difference between the two is massive.

Paul draws this distinction by using the image of putting off the old self and putting on the new self. Paul differentiates between the two:

> You, however, did not come to know Christ that way. Surely you heard of him and were taught in him in accordance with the truth that is in Jesus. You were taught, with regard to your former way of life, to put off your old self, which is being corrupted by its deceitful desires, to be made new in the attitude of your minds; and to put on the new self, created to be like God in true righteousness and holiness. (Ephesians 4:20–24)

We participate in the life of the living Christ through the Holy Spirit whom he sent us. We are not making righteousness happen by believing enough, but we are trusting that the new self created to be like God is something I participate in by the Holy Spirit. The place where the Spirit first goes to work is in my attitude. I continually slide into an attitude of hopelessness because of what is lacking in me. I keep leaving the old self in place and wondering why he doesn't have enough faith to change himself, which leaves me in a place of hopelessness because the old self is not like God and desires mostly deceitful things.

Putting on the new self is putting on Christ. It's kind of an odd way to say it, I suppose, but the image that Paul is using is perfect if we pay attention to what is going on. I put on Christ, in that I am now participating in his life rather than my old life. I don't trust in my faith to make the old life holy. I discard it. I put on the new life, which is the life of Jesus, and the life of Jesus is present with me by his Spirit because Jesus reigns right now in heaven and has brought us into his life by the Spirit. I simply participate in his life.

This sounds really complicated but in actuality is simple, though indeed mysterious. I trust Jesus to be who Jesus is, and I trust that his life is actually alive in me and that I am alive in him. My security is not in my faith or even my experience. It is in Jesus' life. It is in Jesus' ability to be my new self. It is in the Spirit's power to make me a participant in the life of Jesus.

It is Jesus in us who loves, serves, and gives his life away to the world through us. We are participants but he is the leader.

Paul put it this way: "For to me, to live is Christ and to

die is gain" (Philippians 1:21). This relationship with Jesus is so deep and never-ending that Paul could look at impending death and say with boldness that to die is gain. Why would death be gain? Because then his union with Christ would be fully realized. When we die in Christ, a relationship that right now is experienced imperfectly because of our fallen state will be realized in perfection.

For me to live, daily, in each moment, in each relationship, in moments of temptation, in moments of joy, in times of crisis ... is Christ. I trust in his life, and he is allowing me to participate in his life because he has overcome sin and death and ascended into heaven and sent his Spirit. Not by my strength, not by my power, but by his Spirit I participate in the life of our risen King.

Each time I realize how amazing the gospel is it sounds too good to be true.

Each time I realize how amazing the gospel is it sounds too good to be true—to know that God's love for me is secure because Jesus has made it secure; to accept the reality that it's not up to me, but it's up to him; to understand that my faith does not make this happen, but that it has already happened. I am simply asked to pay attention to Jesus and participate in his life. This knowledge gives me security and assurance that his will is being done in my life.

When Jesus ascended into heaven, he not only sent us the Spirit. He also is seated at the right hand of God praying for us. The living Christ is paying attention to our life, and he cares for and is interceding for us.

The writer of Hebrews tells us: "Therefore he is able to save completely those who come to God through him, because he always lives to intercede for them" (Hebrews 7:25).

What an incredible reality. Jesus is the one capable of saving you completely if you come to God through him. Not partially, or for a few years. Not contingent on your ability to behave or believe right. Not on your experience of him or feeling in touch with him. *He* is able to save completely. Our security gives birth to hope, because Jesus creates our assurance of salvation.

When you fail he is praying for you; when you don't get it he is praying for you; when you suffer he is praying for you.

But what is even more incredible is the way he is doing that. "He always lives to intercede for them." It is so crucial that we allow the whole story of the gospel to inform our hearts here. Jesus' death on the cross was essential to our salvation, but the writer of Hebrews tells us that his resurrection and the fact that he is still alive as our great high priest are crucial as well. Jesus is at work in our life daily interceding for us.

The living Christ is relevant to every circumstance we are going through. When you fail he is praying for you; when you don't get it he is praying for you; when you suffer he is praying for you. He is participating in *your* life just as you participate in *his*. He doesn't simply bestow on us an empathetic but powerless smile; instead, he goes to bat for us day and night.

When something bad happens I am tempted to cast off this security. The loss of someone I love, the death of a dream, or an irresolvable conflict—whatever the difficulty, the first question I want to ask is, Where is God? And the second question is, What did I do wrong that this would happen to me? Neither of those questions draws me into the life of Christ. They mostly leave me feeling more alone and more frustrated.

If I could stop for a moment in my pain and really allow my confidence to not be in my circumstances but in the reality of Jesus' complete salvation, then I have a shot at remembering that Jesus is here, bringing my situation before the Father. He is redeeming this pain and causing it to work for good, he is present with me by the Spirit to bring me comfort, and he is victorious even over death.

The relevance of the risen Christ shows up in any situation that we find ourselves in because *he always lives to intercede for us.* I will never enjoy security until I hope in Jesus alone, not in my circumstances. Thankfully he is alive and participating in my life as he intercedes for me *always.*

Jesus himself creates the security that my soul longs for, and that security gives birth to a confident hope because Jesus is completely saving me. Hope causes me to desire Jesus because of all that Jesus is to me.

Jesus is the anchor of my hope.

Someone may protest here because it sounds as though I don't have to work at this. What about our responsibility to obey? What about all the commands that we are called to do? I think the uneasiness that some may feel about placing all of the focus on Jesus and not on us is a fear that we will cheapen grace and just go on sinning because there isn't a negative motivation to not sin. In other words, even if we do sin he will cover for us, so why not just chase after our deceitful desires and let Jesus sort out the mess?

It makes me think of Paul's words: "What shall we say, then? Shall we go on sinning so that grace may increase? By no means!" (Romans 6:1–2).

The real question being asked here is, What is my motivation to seek Christ if Jesus has already secured my salvation? Why would I be anything but complacent if my salvation relies only on his power and not on my faith? It's a good question.

Underneath the question something is being assumed. I think the assumption goes like this: If I am not motivated to seek Christ by the negative consequences of not seeking Christ, then I will never seek Christ.

Once again we are touching on duty rather than desire. What motivates me is a pretty good indicator of what I believe. If I believe my security comes from my own efforts, then I will try hard to become the person Jesus wants me to be. The negative side is that I am motivated by insecurity, not Christ.

But when all the weight of my salvation is placed squarely on Christ, some may fear that we won't have any motivation to obey him. The false assumption is that we obey to prove that our salvation is secure; but the truth is that we obey because Jesus has secured our salvation. We obey as a response to love.

This makes me think about faithfulness in marriage. What motivates a spouse to remain faithful? Is it purely the negative consequences of being unfaithful? When a relationship is unhealthy it is primarily held together by the fear of negative consequences.

"We stayed together for the kids" means that we didn't want to hurt the kids, but we didn't stay together out of love. We were faithful to each other at the lowest level so the kids wouldn't have to endure our divorce. Did these kids get a picture of faithfulness?

When we are primarily motivated to obey only to avoid negative consequences, we are not living into the fullness of love that is ours.

Or "I wouldn't cheat on my husband because I wouldn't want to lose the house and go through a messy divorce, and he has made it clear that it would be very messy if I ever failed him."

These are not pictures of faithfulness based on being secure in the other's love. These are pictures of duty without the security of love. The lack of assurance of unconditional love perverts faithfulness in relationship and creates a relationship held together by fear of negative consequences.

This happens in our relationship with God. When we are primarily motivated to obey only to avoid negative consequences, we are not living into the fullness of love that is ours. We are obeying, yes, but it is a faith that is only staying together for the kids, void of love.

Christ has made his statement of love for us that included the forgiveness for our unfaithfulness. The cross cries out that Jesus knows that you may be unfaithful, but his love for you is unconditional. What motivates you to obey God more? The fear of negative consequences or the reality that Jesus has already forgiven us for our unfaithful acts because he loves us?

What motivates us to be faithful to Jesus is not the fear of negative consequences but the security of Christ's unconditional love.

Jesus lived the perfect human life of worship and Jesus died under the judgment of our sin — essentially he died the death we should have died.

Jesus resurrected from the dead, overcoming sin and death, so that he lives now in a new body animated with eternal life. Jesus gave birth to our new humanity when he conquered death through resurrecting from the dead as a man in a glorified body.

Jesus ascended into heaven and is seated at the right hand of the Father.

Jesus is praying for us day and night.

Jesus is our great high priest who is standing in for us with the Father and advocating on our behalf.

Jesus is mediating the Father's gracious love to us by the Holy Spirit.

The inadequacy in me is obvious; but there isn't any inadequacy in Jesus. My faith falters but Jesus doesn't.

I don't want to sin because I don't desire it in the same way anymore. Instead, I desire the one who loves me and in whom my security rests. I want to be found in him. The negative consequence of sin that I am avoiding is that I don't want to hurt Jesus, the one I love and the one who has loved me and will love me unconditionally.

Sin loses its attraction when we are attracted to Jesus.

I am not trying to avoid losing the house and the kids; I am avoiding sin because I am more attracted to the love of my wife.

Sin loses its attraction when we are attracted to Jesus. Though we won't be perfect in this life, we can continue to be more and more attracted to Jesus as we find ourselves more and more secure in his love.

I don't think we have to live in fear that the goodness of Jesus' love may not be enough of a motivation for us not to sin. Instead I think when we grasp how good the gospel really is and our hearts begin to rest securely in the living Christ, our motivation to participate in the life of Jesus by the power of the Holy Spirit will only grow. This is worship.

The assurance of our faith is not in our faith; it's in Jesus. He lives to send us his Spirit, he lives to intercede for us always, he lives so he can continue to save us, and he lives to bring us into the Father's love.

I pray that you will trust Jesus as your security — who

he is, what he did, where he reigns, the promises he keeps, and the work he accomplished on the cross. The fullness of deity in bodily form. I pray that your security in Jesus gives birth to a hope that dissolves all insecurity and allows you the freedom to receive the fullness of Jesus. And I pray that you will see Jesus exalted and present in your life, and that you would love him because he first loved you.

FORMATION QUESTIONS

1. If your security in Jesus is based on your ability to have enough faith, how secure would you be right now?
2. What relief do you experience knowing that your security rests on the living Christ?
3. How does knowing that Jesus intercedes for you strengthen your faith?
4. How does having your security anchored in Jesus and not your ability to believe bring you hope?
5. What motivates you more, the unconditional love of Jesus for you or negative consequences for disobeying his commands? Explain.

TEN

The Realization of Desire

You are a miracle. It may sound trite, but it's true. Each person created in the image of God bears the value and significance of their Creator. That's why it's so unnerving to see how many people think they don't have much to offer to the kingdom. Have you ever looked at yourself and thought you don't have anything to offer? That you don't have the gifts or the skills that matter? One of the tragedies among the people of God is that we often don't believe that we are a miracle. The God who spoke creation into being created you on purpose, with a unique personality and personhood, and he gifted you to make a mark on other people's lives for his glory. That's amazing and here is why.

If Jesus is the life that we offer to God, his perfect devotion is the response to God we claim for ourselves. But here's our next problem. Because everything is in Christ, we fear we'll lose ourselves altogether and become reduced, less human, depersonalized. It is one thing to lose ourselves in Jesus through communion in his love, but it is another thing to resign ourselves of our personhood and become nothing.

This is not the case. "I praise you because I am fearfully and wonderfully made" was David's cry to God (Psalm 139:14). The love of God is applied to us as unique persons with distinct personhood. Our relationship with Christ is a personal and relational union between two beings that have become one. Christ does not absorb us into a state of non-being; rather, he retains the deepest levels of our personhood and shapes them into the fullest sense of who we were made to be.

Christ is the one through whom and by whom all things were made, including you with all of your particulars. He does not banish our personal desires. Instead, our ultimate desire for Christ, and the experience of his love, gives life to desires that are God-given and God-glorifying. As his love captures our hearts, our desire for sin remains only in the flesh and becomes a lesser desire, disempowered by the Spirit of Christ in us.

Desire is rooted deeply in our personhood and manifested in our personality. Our response to the love of God in Christ is ultimately assisted and made complete by his Spirit. And our personal, unique desires are motivated by and stem from a love for the King.

In your unique personality lie desires God placed within you. You like to make things. You feel happy when you help people. You long for friendship. You want to be known. You like to learn. What you desire is often related to the way that God has gifted you and the purpose for which he gave you those gifts.

Despite whatever weakness exists in those desires, our union with Christ makes up for whatever is lacking so that those desires offered to the King are welcomed and accepted by God with pleasure in his heart toward you. This makes sense since you already belong in the communion of his love.

We live now for the love of the King. For the love of the King, we serve. For the love of the King, we worship and hope and engage his creation with a profound sense that our King reigns in our hearts and has made us for himself.

As we begin to serve, we find the gifts God has given us. Rooted deep within our very beings are those things that bring him glory and give us joy. That passion for art, the quick mind he gave you for numbers, the fulfillment you have in running a company, the energy you get from having people over and making a great meal—all are desires that find meaning in Christ.

But it is easy to question this.

In our churches, it seems, we have only a limited number of gifts that are valued. The person who preaches, the teacher in the class, and the guy leading worship all seem to have gotten the goods, while the rest are left thinking the gifts within us have no place within a worship service or a church event. We are left thinking that these desires are just aspects of our personhood that have no bearing on our spiritual lives.

That's not true.

The things that you are good at and that give you life are all channels for you to live with passion and desire for the love of the King. The love of Christ for us is very personal here. The poet, the painter, and the plumber all have the opportunity to live out their giftedness in their particular area for the love of the King.

The poet, the painter, and the plumber all have the opportunity to live out their giftedness in their particular area for the love of the King.

That which we are passionate about defines us deeply. Apart from Christ, these passions enflame with self-love and become mirages of their intended reality.

Your desire to sing becomes a quest for fame instead of a medium of worship. Your ability to throw great parties becomes a way to get people to praise you instead of creating a space of great hospitality where people's lives connect to one another. Your skills at fixing things are reduced to your job and not an outlet to help others or mentor someone younger. The list can go on and on because we are quick to make our gifts about us and not about Jesus.

For those in the kingdom, however, our gifts are life-giving passions through which Jesus' life is displayed, his kingdom breaking in.

We spend so much energy wishing we were someone else. Don't waste your time on that. Christ has completed the work for us. We are his and he is ours, and in him we rest in triune love. Why waste time thinking we are not sufficient and being jealous over those we think are sufficient? We have already seen that no one is sufficient but Christ, and in him we are brought into union with the Father. That's enough. What can you add to perfect love?

The guy who slugs it out at work every day displays the kingdom when he is living for the love of the King. He is faithful, loves his wife, leads his home, adores his kids, and admits when he fails. You and I will never hear about him, he will never be famous, and some of us would look at his job and think it is not a place you could live with passion. But Jesus has become the object of his desire, and by the grace of Christ he displays the kingdom of peace, mercy, kindness, faithfulness, joy, and purity in every detail of his life. He won't preach a sermon on Sunday, but he will leave a legacy in his home and his workplace, where he did what God made him to do for the love of the King.

The capacity of God to communicate his love is endless. He relates to us all in unique ways that are appropriate to who we are and how we are made.

Sometimes it appears that only certain personalities can make it in the world of religious devotion: the disciplined, Type-A personality that does all the right things in the right way for the right outcome. The truth is there is endless room in the kingdom for all types of personalities. The capacity of God to communicate his love is endless. He relates to us all in unique ways that are appropriate to who we are and how we are made.

God is creative. In order to love us he doesn't call us *out* of our desire but moves us *into* our desire. That means he is working in the realm of our personality and personhood. He uses the creative personality and meets them by his Spirit in their creativity. He does the same for the intuitive person. He meets the extrovert through the lives of other people and the introvert in quiet solitude.

He wants you to become most deeply who he made you to be, and that doesn't require you to be less of yourself but more of yourself. Who you are is key to completing the picture of a beautiful kingdom. He has a meaningful way for you to contribute to the picture as he relates to you in the uniqueness of your own personality.

Being captured by the love of Christ draws us *into* our deepest desires, not *away* from them. United with him, we find that his life begins to pour out of us through the uniqueness of who we are. He loves us personally, he gifted us uniquely, and he shows himself to people specifically through us.

God wants you to become most deeply who he made you to be, and that doesn't require you to be less of yourself but more of yourself.

In the wisdom of God he made you, and in the mercy of God he saved you in Christ so he could love you. And, in loving you, he gives life to you through your passions. Jesus makes up for whatever is lacking.

This means that the kingdom called desire is a place where we experience deep freedom. We are free in so many ways. Free to chase after who we most deeply are. Free from trying to pay God back, and free to rest in the perfected devotion of Jesus. We are free to become more of ourselves, not less of ourselves. Free to pursue the things we love and the things that give us life for the love of the King.

Someone may say at this point that their desires are sinful, yet those are the only desires that truly give them life. Perhaps one person feels it is life-giving to steal from her boss or another person to cheat on his spouse. But the very nature of the outcomes demonstrate that these are not life-giving desires and therefore are not desires that

> **The kingdom called desire is a place where we experience deep freedom.**

are for the King. The cheating spouse destroys another to gain what he calls life. The thief takes so that another loses.

Christ in me sets me free to be who Christ created me to be, and therefore desire will not lead to disappointment. Desires displayed for the love of the King have eternal weight to them, and nothing generated by the life of Jesus will ever die.

We should be careful to understand that the desires in themselves are not the point. They are simply manifestations of a greater desire—our love and need for God—which is why we keep in mind that this is all from him and for him.

Keep one thing in mind, however: Our gifts are meant

to be shared in community, for they can only flourish in relationship to others. Without relationship these gifts turn inward and move us into self-love, and we begin to worship ourselves again. Our gifts can become idols, but in the context of community our gifts are just that—gifts. They are gifts from God to us, for us to give away for others to enjoy. In the kingdom, our gifts and passions move us toward other people for their benefit and God's glory, not our own benefit or our own glory.

It is easy to see how those with leadership gifts could slip up here. Leading a company, making a good living, or climbing the corporate ladder can lead to the temptation of thinking we are in this for our own glory.

Our gifts are meant to be shared in community, for they can only flourish in relationship to others.

But I think of the handicapped person. Or someone with a mental disability. What does he desire? Perhaps just the desire to belong and be treated as though he belongs. He has much to contribute out of the depths of his personhood and even through his weakness, in a community that acknowledges his contributions. His desire to belong draws us together and keeps us from running around under the illusion of our individuality.

What we have to give one another is Christ in us, and what we have to receive from one another is Christ in them. Christ makes up for what we can't do. That means ability, IQ, and worldly success are not the markers we look for, but Christ in us and Christ in the other. So who will carry the burden of the lonely? Who will show up in Jesus' love to include this person? Who will include and value the one for whom the world has no accolades?

What we give out of the depths of our desires is accepted and given life by Jesus in the community of others. This principle is true for the CEO, the writer, the actor, the musician, and the educator, and on and on it goes. What we offer out of the gifts we have received is simply Christ in us, and we offer this to Christ in them — or in the hopes that Christ may be revealed to them. Always in him and for the other.

I have this vision of the people of God that continues to spur me. I see a diverse people, passionate in worship, who are free. They are unburdened and unashamed. They are incredible, imaginative people with great courage. They look peculiar in our world, because they love so powerfully but they don't love for power. They are joyfully living out of their truest selves, and they enjoy being who they are. They have been touched by something that is attractive to others. They pledge allegiance to a King of life and love in a way that is good and true and beautiful. They are not afraid to risk. They are incredibly creative. They put their whole selves into relationships and they bleed love. A limitless flow of good works comes from them. They are full of life, and they enter some of the most painful situations with tenderness and hope. They are honest, courageous, and loving. They don't belong here, the world is not worthy of them, and the world may never recognize them. They have been captured by a vision of another world, and they are sustained by a love that comes from somewhere else. They are Jesus' people. They are the fragrance of life to a dying world and the stench of death to those who have become less than human.

I believe in these people. I believe in you. I believe in us. I believe we are a miracle. Not because of us but because of Jesus in us. What if we were people who were not afraid of what we most deeply desire? Would we find ourselves fulfilled in Christ? Would we have a meaning to our lives that pushes us past the vacant desires of worldly security? In this vision these people risk, they love, they create, they pray, they serve, they proclaim, and they sacrifice. They are a people who have found what their hearts were made for. They are the people of the King in a kingdom called desire. And there are moments, sacred moments, when we are that for the King. They never seem to stick around as long as I wish they would, but for that moment Jesus' people are acting like Jesus because they have realized their desire in him. Those are great moments, and they are meant to show up in us more and more.

FORMATION QUESTIONS

1. What are you good at?
2. What do you love to do?
3. What kind of personality do you have?
4. If you were created by God to live out of your gifts, how can you imagine them being expressed in the kingdom for the love of the King?
5. Would you be more comfortable doing that inside the church or outside the church? Why?
6. What would it take to fulfill those desires?

ELEVEN

Kingdom Identity

In the middle of this dream of a kingdom people is the glaring reality that the church does not really look like this now. We are not people who risk, love, pray, create, serve, proclaim, and sacrifice very well. Church is a very unattractive place for most people. And while countless churches are changing and adapting to become all that they are called to be in the kingdom, countless more are not.

I believe in the church. I believe in the church because the church is Jesus' idea and is essential to the kingdom. We tend to think in terms of relevance or irrelevance. I understand the tension between those two things. When the language our communities speak is foreign to our church culture, there are significant obstacles to doing what we are called to do. If our language does not meaningfully and understandably communicate the reality of Jesus, then we have a problem.

I don't think that is the major issue, though. It assumes

that if we had the right music, preaching, building, and so forth, then people would be highly interested in coming to our programs. Those issues continue to push us into the how-to questions, but they don't tap the deeper issues of desire. What does the church want? What does our community most deeply desire?

The issue of relevance is only a problem because we have failed to engage the culture for such a significant period of time that the culture no longer speaks the same language we do. But the problem exists because at some point we stopped being the church that is displaying the kingdom and instead became a church that is hiding the King in the basement, trying to protect him from the bad world.

This retreating mentality comes from not asking a better question and because we haven't thought critically about the answer to that question. What does the church desire? Do we desire Jesus? We cannot assume the answer is yes. Do we want to display the kingdom and live into the love and life of the King? We retreat from the world because we want some level of protection that we were never called to have. In the kingdom, we are called to be a different type of community: an unprotective one, a courageous and crucified one, a community of Jesus.

I believe in the church. I believe the church is essential. I believe in the essence of the church, which is the people of God, and I believe the church is essential to Jesus' kingdom announcement and reign in the world. I don't believe the issues are music or programming or buildings. I believe the real issue is: *Do we know who we are, and will we be that for the world?*

When I think of the church I think miracle. Sometimes a funky, backwards, stubborn, and sinful miracle, but miracle nonetheless. The church is a community of kingdom people who have come to believe in Jesus, are trusting in Jesus to be their life, are united to Jesus by the Spirit, and have been given very particular gifts, so the community can be who we are called to be for Jesus, each other, and the world. That's miracle. That is not organizationally accomplished. That does not come through a program or a strategy. It is the miracle of being the people of God.

I am captured by Jesus' vision for the church, but sometimes I wish I could break free of it, because being part of a church is hard. I would be lying to say I didn't have those moments when I see how easy it would be to live for Jesus without the church. I would find it much easier to just find a group of friends with whom to live out my faith. But I am brought back by the compelling vision Jesus has for the church, and that vision does not consist of just me hanging out with my friends. Jesus gave us a vision for a diverse community of people who never would have gravitated toward each other on their own, but there they are. They are loving and devoting themselves to one another, because they have Jesus in common. Then

> **When I think of the church I think miracle. Sometimes a funky, backwards, stubborn, and sinful miracle, but miracle nonetheless.**

supernaturally they give themselves away for the sake of the world, in the name of Jesus. They also hurt each other. Sometimes they hurt each other badly. Then in Jesus' vision of the church, they forgive each other, reconcile with one another, and move forward in peace. Apart from miracle that could never happen.

Jesus painted the picture of the church for his followers in Matthew 16:13–19:

> When Jesus came to the region of Caesarea Philippi, he asked his disciples, "Who do people say the Son of Man is?"
>
> They replied, "Some say John the Baptist; others say Elijah; and still others, Jeremiah or one of the prophets."
>
> "But what about you?" he asked. "Who do you say I am?"
>
> Simon Peter answered, "You are the Christ, the Son of the living God."
>
> Jesus replied, "Blessed are you, Simon son of Jonah, for this was not revealed to you by man, but by my Father in heaven. And I tell you that you are Peter, and on this rock I will build my church, and the gates of Hades will not overcome it. I will give you the keys of the kingdom of heaven; whatever you bind on earth will be bound in heaven, and whatever you loose on earth will be loosed in heaven."

After the disciples have followed Jesus for several years,

hearing him teach about the kingdom and seeing him display the kingdom, he initiates something new: the church. Peter's answer to the question, "Who do you say I am?" creates the entry point. Jesus is the Messiah, Israel's King, God's King. This confession of faith is only made possible because God is on the move. God revealed it to him, and the result was the blessing of Peter's salvation.

In this confession and in the person of Peter the church has its origination. The identity of the church comes from the people who are called out by God and have been brought to believe that Jesus is King. That our identity lies in confessing Christ is significant, because without that confession we reduce our understanding of what it means to be the church. We reduce it to some type of program or strategy, and we may even go so far as to believe a lie that we are not the church until we reach a certain size or have all our pieces up and running in the right way.

You are the church if you follow Jesus. You hurt the church if you leave her.

But that's not true. We are the church because Jesus has been revealed to us by the Father. We are the church because we desire Jesus for Jesus' sake, and we confess him as our King. That is our identity. That is who we are. So we can't really leave the church because *we* are the church. The idea of being a follower of Jesus independently of other followers of Jesus is a lie. You can't do that. You can only be someone who is not participating in the life of Jesus' community. To not participate is harmful to the community as a whole, because he gifted you for the common good of the people of God. You are the church if you follow Jesus. You hurt the church if you leave her.

In a culture of consumerism, the issue of relevance gets misappropriated. We are to be relevant for a very simple reason: so we can communicate to the world that Jesus is their King. The people need to hear this in their own language, and it needs to be understandable.

Relevance in a consumer culture assumes church must have something to offer *me*. Instead of seeing church as a community we treat it like a product. The worship service is treated the same way we treat going to a movie: *Did I like it? Did I get anything out of it? I am never going to see that again! Did someone spill popcorn on the floor? I can't believe they're making me stand again! No texting during the show!*

This is really hurtful to the bride of Christ and the vision of Jesus. I think we need to reframe how we see the church. The church is a diverse family of God's people, and in our diversity lies a natural and uncomfortable tension. We don't all get along and we don't all like each other. But we don't get to choose our families. They are chosen for us.

Family can be a hurtful metaphor because not everyone had the greatest family growing up. However, I have come to believe it is the right metaphor. In a family, you don't choose to not be a son because you had a bad time at Thanksgiving. You are a son. You can't change that. You could leave, just like you could leave the church. But the next Thanksgiving would be a sad experience at the table because a son has gone missing.

Relevance doesn't work in family because families are funky. We are who we are for good and bad, and we are placed in our families by God and not by choice. In the same way, Jesus created the community of the church to be a family that comes into being by a new birth in Jesus and the miracle of our union with him. Jesus didn't create a product for us to evaluate and decide if we like it or not, but he created a family that we belong in regardless of how funky this family is. If you're not at the table, the celebration just isn't the same.

We have to come to a place where we lay down our preferences in order to work for the common good. I heard Wendell Berry, a farmer and writer from

> **Jesus didn't create a product for us to evaluate and decide if we like it or not, but he created a family that we belong in regardless of how funky this family is.**

Kentucky, say once that we need to "suffer the community." I like that phrase and I don't like it at the same time. I don't like it because I don't want to be put out by anyone. I don't want to deal with people who are difficult. But I like the phrase because it's so close to the truth.

I believe in the church, and I dream of a day when I have the maturity to suffer the community. I know I can't do it in my own power, which takes me back to church as miracle. I need Jesus to suffer the community in me and through me. You need Jesus to suffer the community through you. We are the people of God called to faith in Jesus our King and born into an amazingly diverse, dysfunctional miracle.

When you think you can't live in the community of God's people any more and you have had enough, you are probably right. But Jesus can do it. He loves those people and you are united to him. Don't be the wife who stays home while the husband goes to the extended family gathering. You go *with* Jesus and *in* Jesus, and you should ask Jesus to help you love these people.

> **When you think you can't live in the community of God's people any more and you have had enough, you are probably right. But Jesus can do it.**

The apostle Paul used marriage as a metaphor for Jesus' relationship with the church. Looking back to Genesis he recounts, " 'For this reason a man will leave his father and mother and be united to his wife, and the two will become one flesh.' This is a profound mystery — but I am talking about Christ and the church" (Ephesians 5:31 – 32).

Jesus united himself to the church. Jesus is one with the church. She is in the process of being made "a radiant church, without stain or wrinkle or any other blemish, but holy and blameless" (Ephesians 5:27).

So if you are leaving the church, you're not really leaving her; you're leaving Christ. Sadly, a large number of the people leaving are the men who are needed to lead and offer themselves to Jesus for the sake of his church. This weakens the church and therefore weakens the kingdom. We will have to answer Jesus when he asks us why we left the bride that he died to create.

The truth is, the church will never meet most of your expectations, and in my opinion the church shouldn't spend a lot of time trying to. The church is supposed to be a place where Jesus is proclaimed and worshiped and where he meets us through Word, sacrament, and prayer. If that's your expectation then you are in luck.

When the church caters to the expectations of the consumer, and the consumer is constantly threatening to leave if his expectations are not met, then we all cease being who we were called to be. We are the people who confess that Jesus is the Christ, the Son of the living God. We are the communion of people who worship

> **The truth is, the church will never meet most of your expectations, and in my opinion the church shouldn't spend a lot of time trying to.**

their King and are sent to display his kingdom. He gave us himself in Spirit, Word, sacrament, prayer, and one another. That is enough.

So we are left with this one difficult calling and blessing, to suffer the community for the glory of the King. We can do this not because we are so good that we will never be irritated by the people in our communities, but because Jesus is using those people to change us. I have to realize that I too am one of those people who needs to be made different by Jesus.

The church is the one place in the world where Jesus'

reign should be unopposed. We live in a world where everyone thinks they are sovereign. This is true at a national level,
a corporate level, and a personal level. We fundamentally
believe no one should be able to tell us what to do. But in the
community of the church we are a people who have bowed
our knee to a good and loving King. We put ourselves under
his reign and renounce our desires to run our own lives and
live out our own agendas. Since he is our King, we can make
room for him in our hearts, allowing him to love the church
through us. He can suffer the community in us. He suffered
the community on the cross, dying for its sins. The church
is his idea, not ours. Jesus tells us that we are the church and
through us the kingdom of heaven is going to be displayed.
So quit bitching about it and start being it. You're embarrassing Jesus.

What does any of this have to do with desire? Desire
is often met in us in a paradoxical way. When we serve the
other we are blessed by the offering. We don't give to get,
but we receive something in the giving that is surprisingly
fulfilling. If Jesus is the object of desire, then to suffer the
community is to suffer Jesus—to love him in the other person, to serve Jesus in them. To do it unto them is to do it
unto him. If you want to see Jesus, if Jesus is the object and
fulfillment of desire, then go to him and love him and serve
him. When you love the church you love him. He is present
in your sister and brother. If you desire Jesus then you will
need to be in relationship with other believers, and you will

need to give yourself to them without expectation of what they will give you in return. Then you will see Jesus. This is who we are in the kingdom of desire.

FORMATION QUESTIONS

1. What is your experience of church?
2. The author tells us that we are the church. If that is the case, are you helping the church or hurting the church?
3. What would it look like for you to "suffer the community" like Wendell Berry talks about?
4. What expectations have you had of church that may be unrealistic?
5. What will it look like for you to use your gifts to love other people knowing that when you love them you love Christ?

TWELVE

Kingdom Vocation

The church is the one place where Jesus' kingship is unopposed. He is the head of the church, and we are his people who live under his reign. He has entrusted us with a very specific vocation. He has given us the keys to the kingdom, keys that unlock heaven and allow it to break in on earth. The church displays to the world what the kingdom of heaven is like when it shows up on earth. We unlock the kingdom by announcing to the world that Jesus is the world's King too and that he is restoring all creation through Jesus.

This is an invitation to imagine. What would it look like if the kingdom broke into your life? What does it mean in your family, your city, and your church? As we have already seen, when the King arrives in our hearts and unites us to himself by his Spirit, deep inner transformation takes place. We are more attracted to the Savior than we are to sin. We are brought into the life and love of the King. Our deepest desires are fulfilled in Jesus.

That transformation is the center of world transformation. Out of the depths of our renewed desires Jesus sends us into the world to announce his reign. We are invited to imagine what the world looks like under the reign of Jesus and get to work unlocking the reality of heaven. The church's vocation stems from her identity. We are the people of Jesus and therefore we display his life wherever he calls us.

The people of God are taking part in a quiet revolution. Gradually and sometimes unseen, the kingdom is growing and breaking in all around us. We are called to help people discover the love of the King, and many times their first taste of this love is through us. Jesus loves the world and we are the vehicles love flows from. We don't wait for our personal transformations to be finished to go out and display the love of the King. We simultaneously experience the Spirit of God changing us and drawing us into those places of desire while we go out and offer that love to others.

> **The people of God are taking part in a quiet revolution. Gradually and sometimes unseen, the kingdom is growing and breaking in all around us.**

Imagination is so crucial here because our world is broken. We don't see the display of heaven on the nightly news. So we are called to dream about what the kingdom looks like in the dire issues our communities face, such as poverty, addiction, and the sex trade. What does the kingdom of heaven look like in the midst of business and education? In the midst of moviemaking or sports, politics or agriculture? In the midst of educating our children or caring for our elderly?

In *all* areas of culture, kingdom people are sent to live into their calling, which is to be the worshiping people of the King, those who display the love of his reign. So here in the midst of very specific problems we are invited to dream of the King's response to the painful and at times sinful circumstances that are devastating people.

One group of kingdom people imagined what it would look like if the kingdom broke into the health care crisis, where millions of Americans can't get the medical and dental care they need for their families. They imagined what it would look like if doctors, nurses, and dentists came out and offered free clinics in the community. That dream became a reality when they developed free health clinics. Some really gifted administrative people came along and helped with organizing those clinics.

The result was that hundreds of people came out and received the medical and dental care they couldn't afford for themselves or their children. These kingdom people spent the day displaying the love of the King to those who had been left out in the cold. They brought healing into a culture that was creating sickness. As the workers healed and served, they would offer to pray with people they were serving, and many were happy to receive not only medical or dental care, but the loving prayers offered up to our reigning King on their behalf.

The clinics continue to grow in number, and lots of

churches are jumping on board to care for people in our community. Here is where the love of the King and the brokenness of the world collide and the kingdom shows up.

Vocation is central to understanding the role of the church in building the kingdom. Doctors, nurses, and dentists, gifted by the Spirit, come into a new understanding of what they were created for. They are not given those gifts just to have a job and make a living. Their vocation is so much bigger. They are kingdom people first and foremost whose desire to bring healing was given them by God. They didn't simply come up with the idea to become doctors, nurses, or dentists on their own. These were God-given desires that have become God-given vocations. These desires were central to their personalities. These desires bring them joy and pay the bills. And here in the kingdom their desires become a key to unlocking heaven on earth, so the greatness of our King is displayed to the world.

Here is where the love of the King and the brokenness of the world collide and the kingdom shows up.

What we love to do is significant. We may be tempted to think of our work or passions as "nonspiritual," but I don't believe that. I think those desires that move us toward our vocation are central to the kingdom. When we take what we were made to do and what gives us joy and imagine how God could use that to display his kingdom, the result is heavenlike.

Community is a central piece to this. I think that is why

the church is such an amazing thing. Jesus calls us to offer the best of who we are to each other. A group of people daring enough to imagine how they could display the kingdom through their passions and gifts is a vital tool in the hands of the King.

When the doctors, nurses, and dentists connect with the pastors, social workers, and administrators, then something is created that didn't exist before. In the midst of the medical crisis, the Spirit takes these gifted people and creates a portable medical clinic that is changing lives both physically and spiritually.

The great thing about a missional imagination is that the Spirit of God has an endless supply of ideas. There are no limits to how he may use his gifted people in displaying the reign of Christ in the world. When the people of the King surrender their personal vocations to the King, then the church's primary vocation of displaying Jesus to the world makes it an unstoppable force.

> **The Spirit of God has an endless supply of ideas. There are no limits to how he may use his gifted people in displaying the reign of Christ in the world.**

The keys to the kingdom are in our hands. You have been entrusted with them — hard to believe but it's true. We get to invite the world to trust Jesus as their King, and they get to taste his love through the inbreaking reign of the kingdom, flowing through his people.

This changes our position in the world and how we understand our careers. The church's vocation is not to sit on the sidelines of culture and evaluate it, nor is it to try to create an alternate culture that is a cleaned-up version of the dominant culture. Instead we are sent to create a different world. One that displays Jesus as the world's King.

This should create a different set of bottom lines for us as we go off to work. What could the world look like if the church understood her vocation this way Monday through Saturday? In what ways would that change how you understood your vocation? In what ways can you offer your gifts to Jesus and imagine with others how his kingdom might break into your world?

This requires something of our spiritual lives. We can't sit back passively and assume the church is a bunch of programs that take place in a building. We can't assume paid professionals are doing the ministry of the church while we go off to work. We have to become very much aware again of our identity — that we are the church and this is our vocation. This is *my* vocation.

This is what you were made for: to live into the love of the King and display his kingdom through the church in whatever forms that takes.

You are the powerful force of the kingdom, made for the King and offered to the world. I know it doesn't feel like it most days, and perhaps it doesn't even make sense to you. Why would Jesus give us the keys to the kingdom? Not because we are so wise or good. In fact, it is through our weakness that Christ is glorified. He is building his kingdom through mundane and ordinary people. He displays heaven on earth in the ordinariness of you showing up and doing your job, raising your family, and loving your spouse.

Imagining the advance of the kingdom pushes us back into the community. In order for me to experience this miracle with any depth, I will need to imagine what the kingdom could look like, and I will need others to help me do that. I will want to sit with others and ask the questions: What is Jesus inviting us to? What dream is he asking us to imagine? Where is the kingdom being displayed and how can we get in on that?

Why would Jesus give us the keys to the kingdom? Not because we are so wise or good. In fact, it is through our weakness that Christ is glorified.

When Jesus was teaching Peter back in Matthew 16, he not only gave him a kingdom identity for the church and a kingdom vocation for the church, but he also painted a picture of a kingdom destiny. He said the gates of hell, or of Hades, would not prevail against it (Matthew 16:18).

I always thought of that as a defensive posture. Like hell is coming after us and consuming people, but the gates won't be able to lock me up and hold me in. But that is not what Jesus is talking about.

Walls were built around cities in the days of Jesus to keep the enemies out. During attack the enemy forces knew if they could break down the city gates they could breach the walls and sack the city. The army inside the city would fight with everything they had to keep the gates from failing, because they knew once the gate gave way, the city would be taken.

Jesus is telling Peter that the church is playing offense, not defense. We are the ones sacking the city of the kingdom of darkness. We are the great army of kingdom people who are pounding on the gates of hell with love, truth, and justice. We are surrounding the city of darkness — albeit slowly and gradually. With each act of love, motivated by the Spirit of Jesus, we deliver another blow to the city gate. Each time we share with someone that Jesus is Lord, the gates takes a blunt hit and the enemy's strength gives way a little more.

While we look into the kingdom of darkness and see the horrors of abuse, addiction, greed, violence, infidelity, immorality, and the rest of it, Jesus wants to assure us: *That won't be the way it always is.* The kingdom is coming; I've given you the keys. Don't let up. Hell can't stop us. The church prevails, and hell loses.

When you are tempted to stay safe and think that if you cower inside the walls of the church the world won't get you, repent. That's not the church, and you're not living into the identity Jesus gave you.

Next time you're tempted to go to work and climb the corporate ladder so you can get what you want out of the world, repent. That's not why Jesus gave you those gifts and talents. You're not living into the vocation Jesus gave you.

Next time you want to quit loving and serving and giving yourself away for the sake of the kingdom, remember: you're playing offense, not defense. Hell will give way to heaven. Death will give way to life; we know it is true because it has already come true in Jesus, who conquered hell through his own death and brought heaven to earth through his resurrected life.

Here we begin to understand that in Jesus we are being made free. Freedom is central to desire, and we are made most free from fear. If by faith we can accept the miracle of what Jesus is doing in the church, then we are free to be a courageous and dangerous people. When I don't fear other people I am free to embrace them and love them without expectation, because I am loving Jesus in them.

When I don't fear work, then I am free to see my vocation as a gift to build Christ's kingdom. When I don't fear failure, I am free to imagine and dream because my outcomes have been made secure in Jesus. The church is free to be the unified, creative, courageous, unleashed, and sent people of God into the world. God's people will testify with their lives and proclaim with their mouths that Jesus is the King of the world. He reigns today, reconciling the world and giving new life to all who confess him as their God.

FORMATION QUESTIONS

1. In what ways could you imagine the kingdom of heaven breaking in through your gifts?
2. Who do you know that you could imagine with?
3. What does it mean to you that we are the ones breaking down the gates of hell and they won't prevail against us?
4. How could your vocation become a vehicle for kingdom transformation?

THIRTEEN

What Time Is It?

I heard N. T. Wright speak once, and he said there are three questions we should be asking ourselves: Who are we? Where are we? And what time is it?

I think those are important questions we should be wrestling with all the time. I want to focus attention on the last question because I think we find ourselves at a critical moment for being God's people in the world and we need to understand what time we are in.

When God moves among a community of people, everything changes. When God was on the move in Acts, at the first gathering of the church, the Spirit of God shows up, the gospel is announced, people respond by repentance and faith, and the kingdom is displayed.

What marks a person who has been touched by the kingdom? I think the marks of God's movement are the same today as it was for the people of God in the book of Acts. I see six major characteristics:

1. We passionately love Jesus, each other, and our world.
2. We pray because everything depends on Jesus.
3. We celebrate like people who will live forever in the love of our triune God.
4. We serve others because they are worthy of it.
5. We proclaim with power and boldness that God is King of the world in Jesus.
6. We sacrifice our lives for the mission of Jesus because it was the mission of Jesus to sacrifice his life for us.

In other words:

We love.
We pray.
We celebrate.
We serve.
We proclaim.
We sacrifice.

These characteristics of the newly formed church in the book of Acts have been true of God's people throughout history all the way to the present day. All over the world God is moving, and in the wake of God's Spirit a changed community of people love, pray, celebrate, serve, proclaim, and sacrifice. These six characteristics are not all there all the time or even to the fullest extent, but they exist as a response to the movement of God through the gospel.

The question I want to return to then is this: What time is it?

In our time God is moving, creating communities of people who are known for their love, prayers, celebration, service, proclamation, and sacrifice—not as works to earn their way to God but as the liberating response to their desire for Jesus. I believe God's Spirit is working all over the world, across ethnic, economic, denominational, and theological lines, redefining what matters most to the church.

Because God is at work, I think the dominant conversation needs to change in the evangelical world. Too much effort is being expended on questions that have been around for a long time:

Who's in and who's out?

Who's right and who's wrong?

Who's safe and who's dangerous?

Of course theological lines always need to be drawn. People will certainly be attracted to certain theological camps based in their biblically rooted conscience. And of course we do need to be concerned about heresy. Heresy is always dangerous.

But for centuries the church has lived within creeds and confessions that have helped us understand the boundaries of our beliefs, like the Apostles' Creed and the Nicene Creed. We also have clear lines drawn denominationally, with churches writing down confessions or catechisms to help their members understand what they believe. Creeds, confessions, and catechisms. We have no lack of lines to draw. The better question theologically is, What are the boundaries of orthodoxy? I think a lot of peace could be made if we thought that through.

It seems to me that the conversation needs to change from trying to figure out who is in or out. Instead we should be paying attention to the movement of the Spirit among God's people. We are too often tempted to question the fruit of God's movement if it occurs outside our theological comfort zone. Yet we can hardly argue with the fruit of love, prayer, service, celebration, proclamation, and sacrifice in the name of Jesus. Jesus said we will know where he is based on the fruit we see. If Jesus is the object of our desire, then the fruit that follows will be his righteousness, not ours.

The conversation needs to change from trying to figure out who is in or out. Instead we should be paying attention to the movement of the Spirit among God's people.

The controversy over the emerging church has had a paralyzing effect on the church. This new thing that appeared on the scene in the West in the last ten or so years is causing quite a stir, and everyone quickly wants to put a label on it.

Emerging church is a term that has been used for a long time in the study of missions. If we said there is an emerging church in China, we would probably not get freaked out and wonder what in the world those people are doing. But in the West, this new movement being referred to as the emerging church causes concern because in some extreme aspects of it there is heresy. But God *is* moving. His church is emerging in our time and place, and it is a movement of his Spirit, not simply the concoction of a handful of popular leaders who don't tend to agree with each other. We tend to focus on what these popular leaders are writing and saying; then we pick teams and go to war.

But here is the secret to our time: God's movement is happening among *all* the teams. No team gets to claim they win. The church is emerging, renewing, and starting afresh inside the movement of God and across many of the lines that have defined us in our organized camps. The movement of God breaks through and across these lines and unites people who are defined by their desire for Jesus, not their differences.

> **God's movement is happening among *all* the teams. No team gets to claim they win.**

I love sitting down with someone who differs with me theologically on specific issues, not orthodoxy. When I hear the stories of God's Spirit moving among a group of people that are so different than my group, doing things that are beautiful and redemptive in ways I would never imagine myself doing them, I am inspired and humbled. When I think of the way a community church in our town responded to the crisis of Hurricane Katrina, I am blown away. I am amazed by the group of people that are stirring a movement of prayer in my city. I am humbled by the woman at the Baptist church who has been faithful to God for twenty-eight years, teaching the junior high kids at their church. They are experiencing the movement of God. They love people, they pray like everything depends on it, they celebrate the goodness of God in a world of sin and suffering, they proclaim that Jesus is King of the world and the giver of grace through faith, and they sacrifice themselves for the love of King and kingdom. They agree that there is no other hope outside the saving work of Christ.

God *is* moving, and I don't think the key voices of evangelical pop culture have cornered the market on what God is actually creating that is new and fresh in our time. The kingdom is growing and breaking in among us, but many times it goes unnoticed, because the moment controversy arises we turn our eyes away from what the Spirit is doing.

Evangelicals are full of fear, which is a surprising thing since we preach a gospel of freedom. But this community greatly fears being *wrong*, being on the wrong team. After years of thinking it was our job to decide who gets into heaven and who stays out, we experience the residual effects of paralyzing fear. We seem to think that if we don't have our theology spot on, then we may be on the team that goes to hell. It is not our correct doctrine that saves us, though; Jesus saves us.

All this fear is to our peril. God is moving and we may be missing it. We may be afraid of it because he moves in a way we are not used to—a way that is too reformed for our liking, or perhaps too charismatic for us, or in a way that causes too much social engagement. This all keeps us in a state of fear.

This fear is terribly misplaced. Instead of fearing those whose doctrinal stripe is a different color we should fear missing the movement of God because we were paying attention to the wrong conversation. We should fear spending our whole lives creating a fantasy baseball team that never really gets into the game.

We should fear living lives defined by endless judging; prayer that is token, obligatory, and passionless; dull and selfish worship; avoidance of facing the sinful and broken things in us and around us in our world; and lives of religious ease. We should be afraid that our lives could be outside the kingdom called desire. We should fear that we desire being right instead of desiring Jesus.

God is moving among us and in our time, and people are discovering that their deepest desires are being met in Jesus, while his kingdom of love is driving out the fear of man. People are rising up with creative and imaginative ways of being God's people in the world. The Spirit of God is bringing forth new life in those and through those who are being defined by Jesus for the sake of the kingdom.

We should fear that we desire being right instead of desiring Jesus.

What is quite freeing is that movements of the Holy Spirit tend to be uncomplicated. They happen because people focus on the essentials: Jesus and worship. Those joining the movement freely express the mission in ways appropriate and unique to their gifting and personhood. They trust Jesus personally as King and Savior and they understand God's hope for the world. So they suffer and endure willingly for the cause of Christ.

Which means that once we know what time it is, then we have to ask if we are willing to enter into the depths of this kingdom desire, so that we can become people who are defined by the movement of the Spirit.

To say it more simply, do we have the courage to risk what *is* because we are compelled to participate in what *will be* for the glory of Jesus our King?

This is our time. God is on the move. His kingdom is breaking in. His Spirit is transforming us in the depths of who we are. A new world is emerging through the Spirit's leading in God's people. We are leaving our fear behind, and in our joy we are giving our lives away to gain the King and his kingdom, because we desire him. Slowly, piece by piece and step by step, we are experiencing life in a kingdom called desire.

We are leaving our fear behind, and in our joy we are giving our lives away to gain the King and his kingdom, because we desire him.

In Jesus' kingdom our deepest joy confronts our greatest fears to open us up to the unlimited possibilities of living into the life of Jesus and his kingdom.

So . . . what do *you* want?

FORMATION QUESTIONS

1. A kingdom called desire wants you to tap into your desires and not hide from them. In what ways has that happened?

2. In what ways has the freedom of the gospel of Jesus allowed you to rethink your faith?

3. When you think of the six marks of people in the kingdom, do they describe you? How so?

4. Do you resonate with the idea that we spend too much time fearing that we are wrong and not enough time discovering where Jesus is displaying his kingdom? Why do you think that is?

5. Finally, in remembering all that God has done for you in Jesus, as Jesus, and through Jesus, what do you want now?

Acknowledgments

There is always an amazing team of people behind every book. I want to thank that great community of people, as well as the elders and staff of Imago Dei Community who continue to live out Jesus' gospel with boldness and courage. Thanks to Ron Frost, who has mentored me for years in theology and whose love for Jesus continues to inspire me to be faithful. I was greatly helped by his PhD dissertation "Richard Sibbes' Theology of Grace and the Division of English Reformed Theology." I hope that someday this will be published for others to benefit from such great work and fruitful labor.

I was deeply impacted by the works of Andrew Purves, as well as T. F. Torrance, and am indebted to their scholarship and insight.

Thanks to Chris Ferebee, who is a friend and my agent, and the good people at Zondervan, who worked hard to make my thoughts clear and more helpful to the reader. Thanks to my assistant Cait Davis, whose selfless efforts and service have benefited my ministry a ton, and this book is no exception. Also thanks to my faculty colleagues at Multnomah Biblical Seminary—it has been great getting to serve with all of you.

I want to say a special thanks to Aaron James for his work on the cover design. I always appreciate your creativity, which captures things from an interesting and artistic perspective that reflects the ethos of our community and city.

As always, thanks to my family and friends for their encouragement, love, and support—especially my wife, Jeanne, who helped read over my manuscripts more times than she probably likes and always makes them better with her insight and honesty. And thank you to my four children—Kaylee, Josh, Zach, and Bryce. You put the joy in my life.

Thanks to our great God, who is Father, Son, and Spirit, for accomplishing such an amazing salvation for a sinful man like me; I am always amazed at your tenacious love.

I hope that God will speak to your heart out of this book the things that are true and worthy of his name and the rest will be forgotten.

Rick McKinley
Portland
November 2010

Share Your Thoughts

With the Author: Your comments will be forwarded to the author when you send them to *zauthor@zondervan.com*.

With Zondervan: Submit your review of this book by writing to *zreview@zondervan.com*.

Free Online Resources at

www.zondervan.com

Zondervan AuthorTracker: Be notified whenever your favorite authors publish new books, go on tour, or post an update about what's happening in their lives at www.zondervan.com/authortracker.

Daily Bible Verses and Devotions: Enrich your life with daily Bible verses or devotions that help you start every morning focused on God. Visit www.zondervan.com/newsletters.

Free Email Publications: Sign up for newsletters on Christian living, academic resources, church ministry, fiction, children's resources, and more. Visit www.zondervan.com/newsletters.

Zondervan Bible Search: Find and compare Bible passages in a variety of translations at www.zondervanbiblesearch.com.

Other Benefits: Register yourself to receive online benefits like coupons and special offers, or to participate in research.

ZONDERVAN.com/
AUTHORTRACKER
follow your favorite authors